Working In The

Northwest

Woods

WORKING IN THE NORTHWEST WOODS

Dennis Willard

Working In The Northwest Woods
A Personal History

ISBN 978-1466388895

For Suzanne, who supported and encouraged me well beyond what a reasonable person would endure.

Contents

Introduction

I grew up on the thin edge of the great eastern hardwood forest. Not far to the west, the grasslands of the Great Plains took over, but in Southern Missouri, where I spent my youth, the woods were found in compact patches of what people would generally refer to as a woodlot. Farmers cleared the land on most of the small farms that dominated the rural countryside, and then fenced and cross-fenced the fields that supported a variety of grain crops and cattle. Almost every farm had some small section of land still in timber, if only to provide warming firewood for the often bitterly cold winters. Those areas of real woods that did exist were small collections of hickory and oak mostly, with dozens of other species scattered into the mix. The locals made little use of hackberry, elm, and sweet gum even though they grew everywhere. There was walnut, prized for its valuable nuts and beautiful wood. Cherry yielded its delicious fruit and a wood that deep in the center was nearly as red as the fruit. But mostly it was oak. Red oak, white oak, black oak, post oak, and more; difficult at times to tell apart and yielding different fruits that appealed to different birds and small mammals as well as providing beautiful furniture to the individual hearty enough to work his tools through the hard grain of this wonderful wood.

At one time, large portions of this land of ancient mountains where I grew up were covered with vast stands of woods. Pockets of eastern red cedar could be found along the ridges of the Ozark

Mountains, the soil so thin and poor that it could not support the thirstier hardwoods but could provide just enough of a roothold and just enough water for the cedars and their resident ticks to survive. The hardwoods filled the bottoms and river valleys.

My parents traveled little when I was a child so I did not see much of this country until I reached high school and could drive myself. Back then, forty-seven years ago, the farther south I traveled, the fewer farms I encountered and the fewer people I met and the more forest I discovered. Those few people that were there were as tough as the country, most having survived the dust bowl, which touched this country. When they did manage to scrape together a farm, it was as unique and rough-edged as were the residents. They would somehow find enough soil in one place to grow a few vegetables. They cleared what lowland they could find and planted it to corn and grass for the cows and goats they kept. The many spring-fed rivers of this country ran pure and clear and provided habitat for trout in the cool spring outflows, but the water quickly warmed to temperatures more suited to bass and perch. By the time I began exploring the area as a teenager, much of that country, most of it in fact, had been altered in one way or another either by the hardscrabble farmers or by the U.S. Army Corps of Engineers. The Corps built a collection of dams that created a series of warm water reservoirs which lay alongside the now famous country music town of Branson.

The region had already been long settled those many years ago, but it still held much of the original landscape undamaged and unchanged from its beginnings. It was in this country, with its limestone ledges and cedar and pine covered uplands, honeycombed underneath with caves known and unknown that I learned to love the land.

When I arrived in the Northwest in 1969, I was a guest of the United States Navy. As I traveled west from Missouri for the first time, I saw things I could hardly believe. First, the endless miles of grassland that covered Kansas and most of Colorado, then the Rockies with their peaks so high that even at the start of summer they were buried with snow. The real surprise, however, lay ahead of me at the edge of the continent where I saw the Pacific Ocean and Puget Sound with the mountains of the Cascades and the Coast Ranges rising seemingly directly out of the water. Looking at the extent of wild, wooded country I saw before me, the beauty overwhelmed me.

After finishing with my naval service, I found my way back to the Ozark Mountain country for my schooling. I returned to the Northwest in 1976 with a newly issued degree from one of Missouri's state universities. The scholars under whom I had studied proclaimed me a manager of wildlife and a purveyor of the ethics of conservation. I accepted a job with the United States Forest Service working on the Monte Cristo Ranger District of the Mt. Baker-Snoqualmie National Forest. I did so after being unable to shake the memories of my time spent living on the land along the Sound, causing me to embark on this adventure with virtually no thought to direction, goals, or expectations. I only knew I wanted to be surrounded by the beauty and wildness of those mountains that haunted my thoughts. I walked into the ranger station on that first day with no notion of what it was I would be doing or where it would lead me. I also unknowingly walked in on the end of an era.

The end of the days of free-for-all logging and road building had already been decided by popular opinion and by the growing lack of timber, but at the time I was youthfully unaware of most of the details of this philosophical change. Fortunately, for me, I entered the Service when there were still a few employees left who could remember the Forest Service from the "old days". I am not referring to the really old days, of course. Not 1910 or 1920 - that is a subject for another story - but the post-World War II days when there seemed to be no end to the good timber and ambitious loggers scraped miles and miles of road into the sides of mountains to gain access to the valuable stands of fir and cedar and hemlock that waited there.

"Just goin' to waste if we don't cut it out" they would explain.

While I was in school and later working for the Forest Service, the impact of the social and environmental changes that came to this country were largely unclear to me at the time. Mostly I was thinking about adventure, music, and the things that still seem to preoccupy young men's minds. Changes were altering a lifestyle that had defined a large percentage of work in the Northwest. Ultimately, this lifestyle was all but eliminated. While I was largely unaware of it at the time, reflection has served to clarify much of this for me.

With these thoughts, I offer a few essays and recollections that look back on the nine years that I spent working in the woods. Driving the logging roads, walking the trails, laying hose and digging fire line, crawling through the unpleasant underbrush, always wet and mostly always surrounded by bugs, I never imagined that what I was doing would end up being an experience worth sharing with others. It also seems to me now that all of that wet brush and all of those mosquitoes and black flies were not quite as unpleasant as they seemed to me at the time.

Black Bear Lodge
Lake Wenatchee, Washington

Old Growth – It All Started Here

For a hundred years, a thousand years or a hundred thousand years, for as long as the ice has scraped down to bedrock and the sun has melted that ice back to water, the trees of the Northwest have managed to survive. Cold and snow, rain and flood, lightning and fire have all tried to remove them. Most recently, man has tried the same thing, at least European man, but the trees continue to grow. They continue the struggle to survive.

Pushing water up two hundred feet and more to the needles to power the miracle of energy created from the sun, these trees resisted all efforts to overcome their will to endure. The forests survived the onslaught of ice and wind and water and fire until the all-out assault began in the early 1800s with the arriving settlers and their axes and saws.

No one knows exactly how much of the Northwest was covered in old-growth timber at the time the first Europeans arrived. It might be fair to speculate that pretty much everything was timbered, other than the rock and glacier covered mountain summits and of course, the dry interior regions, but that would not take into account the activities of the native inhabitants. They cut a few trees, using red cedar for canoes and for building their wooden houses. Beginning with the Haida people from the Queen Charlotte Islands, over time most of the

Coastal First Nations people carved elaborate totem poles, also from the wood of the cedar. All this activity resulted in the harvest of relatively few trees simply because the number of people was not that large. However, there were also activities related to using fire as a clearing tool, or in some cases fire as a weapon of war. There is a story, passed through oral tradition, that tells of a fire started in 1800, probably by the Cowlitz tribe, which consumed a quarter of a million acres covering what is now the Centralia area all the way to Mount Rainier and Mount St. Helens. In spite of such events as this, and regardless of the actual, and unknowable, historical acreage covered with big and old trees, it is certain there is much less today.

Along the Northwest coast, from Northern California to Alaska, First Nations people lived in a reasonably sustainable relationship with the forests growing from high in the mountains all the way to the water's edge. The names of these people are less well known than those of the Plains Indians and Southwest Indians. Along the wet and heavily forested coast lived the Salish, the Nootka, the Kwakiutl, Bella Coola, Tsimshian, Haida, and the Tlingit. Other groups lived farther inland from the coast. All had one thing in common, that of having a rather minor impact on the natural systems at work in the Northwest forests. Other than the items detailed previously, there existed a comfortable balance between the relatively small populations of humans and the large population of timber. This seems to have been the case regardless of any particular perspective these people had toward nature. It was mostly that the volume of timber and land was large enough to mitigate most human activity, with the exception, of course, of events like the aforementioned fire of 1800.

Any discussion of Northwest old-growth forest must first take into account the understanding of the phrase "old growth". There is no age specific definition of the phrase other than in general descriptive terms. For any given region, it may be possible to define more age details as they relate to species composition and climate, but at its most generic, the term refers to "big, old trees". The best description of old growth is that of a stand of timber which is past the mature age of the most dominant species in that stand. Considering that Northwest forests consist of a mix of western red cedar, western hemlock, Douglas-fir, a few other examples of the "true" firs and a smattering of other species, maturity may vary even from valley to valley as the species mix changes. Elevation would also effect these definitions in the same way. What is common in an old-growth stand is the presence of a number of dead snags, evidence of the maturity of the stand, and an area that can be classified as undisturbed, meaning in most cases, having never been logged.

In the case of the vast burned area from the Cowlitz fire mentioned earlier, the forest that eventually returns to that area would not be considered old growth, but rather successional forest. At some point, of course, for instance now that two hundred years have passed, if it were left alone that area would present all the evidence of being an old-growth forest as the dominant species of the area reached maturity and took on the characteristics of a mature stand once again.

Therefore, in terms that might be outside normal human lifespan measurements, but considerably less than geological timeframes, old growth can come and it can go, and then it can come again.

This all fits nicely into a quietly stable cycle that considered human interaction from the First Nations as they cut and burned, as well as lightning caused fires and windstorms and even the occasional earthquake or volcanic eruption. Areas, sometimes vast areas, were altered by natural events and then recovered in whatever time was needed. Then, the Europeans and Americans arrived.

It was this infusion of wanderers from across the continent and from across the oceans that finally opened the door for the still ongoing conflict between humanity and the timber of the Northwest. In 1774, Spanish sailors on the *Santiago* sighted and named what we now call Mount Olympus on the Olympic Peninsula. A year later, another Spanish expedition landed men on the Washington coast and claimed the land for Spain. The local Quinault Indians, taking exception to this event, engaged in a skirmish that left several dead on both sides. The Spaniards retreated – an ominous beginning. During that same decade, another traveler from European visitors – smallpox – reduced the native population in Western Washington to about 26,000 after killing more than 10,000 people.

Captain James Cook arrived in 1778 for a look around followed by even more English explorers when Captains Robert Gray and George Vancouver visited separately in the 1790s. Vancouver, in particular, was poetic in his description of the timber he saw along the shores of Puget

Sound and areas north, which he called "luxurious" as well as several other florid descriptions. One commonality of all the European explorers of this period was their astonishment at the number and size of the trees they saw along the shorelines.

In these earliest of times, there was little impact on the forests from the Europeans. They did prize the trees for their use as masts and spars for the sailing ships. The wood was tight grained and light, and often free of limbs for a hundred feet. In 1850, a British ship, *Albion*, was seized by a U.S. Customs inspector after he discovered 18 massive pilfered trees aboard that were bound for the Royal Navy. This is likely the first case of known timber thievery in the Northwest. Word was being passed of the spectacular and valuable wood to be found in the forests along the Northwest Coast and folks were showing up to claim it.

Within the old-growth forest are several species of trees, many capable of growing to impressive size and many quite valuable. These trees can be divided into hardwoods, which are the deciduous trees, and softwoods, which we know as the evergreens. Let's examine the hardwoods first.

Unlike those eastern forests of my youth, there is not an abundance of commercially valuable species of hardwoods in the Northwest. There are three types of native maple, big leaf maple, vine maple, and Douglas maple. The latter two differ only in which side of the Cascade Mountains they are found, with the vine maple on the west side. Big leaf maple is a tree that grows to about eighty feet and is used for furniture and for fuel. Vine and Douglas are most commonly smaller trees that make up a lot of the understory of the forests on both sides of the Cascades.

The largest hardwood is black cottonwood, sometimes as tall as one hundred and twenty feet or more, slightly smaller east of the Cascades. It is used mostly for pulp for making paper and as a veneer finish. Red alder is also used in furniture and is very common on the west slopes of the mountains. A smaller relative of red alder, slide alder is found mostly in rocky slide areas, hence the name. Although very uncommon, Oregon white oak also provides wood for furniture.

There are some specialty hardwood trees found in these forests as well. Pacific yew has long been used for wooden archery bows and for fence posts. Recently the drug Taxol has been isolated from the yew and is used in cancer therapy with some success. It is unfortunate that much of the yew had been destroyed prior to this discovery – a strong case for species preservation. Cascara provides a bark that is used as a laxative but the wood of this forty-foot tall tree is not used commercially.

Making up the rest of the old-growth hardwood forest are several species of willow, bitter cherry, black hawthorn, hackberry and Pacific dogwood. Painting the mountain hillsides in the fall are the yellow gold leaves of the paper birch and the quaking aspen.

The really big players in the Northwest woods, Vancouver's "luxurious" forests, are the softwoods. The king of all these trees is the Douglas-fir. Growing to over two hundred feet tall and as much as fifteen feet in diameter, this tree represents the most valuable tree in the forest. This is the lumber tree that has made logging what it is today, with the wood being used for all types of construction. Also valuable is the western red cedar used for decking and roofing and siding, the wood incredibly resistant to decay. This is the tree of the First Nation's history and remains much sought after today. Not as tall as the Douglas-fir, at one hundred fifty to two hundred feet, it usually is found in two or three foot diameters. Much of the original cedar has been removed – a sad testament to the value of the tree.

A collection of other big trees are also valuable lumber producers – Engelmann spruce, grand fir, noble fir, and pacific silver fir are all used for lumber and pulp and are tall trees – from one hundred and twenty to two hundred feet – with diameters up to six feet. Included in this collection one also finds Sitka spruce. This was the tree of choice for the old sail powered mariners who used this light, strong wood for masts and spars. It was also valuable during the early days of aviation as a lightweight structural wood for airplanes. Western hemlock, western larch and Alaska cedar, sometimes called yellow cedar, are also much sought after.

Found mostly on the drier, east side of the Cascade Mountains or along the coastline at beach level, the Northwest pines include the lodgepole, which is known as shore pine when found along the seacoasts, and the western white pine which has largely disappeared from the west side forests due to white pine blister rust. The king of the pines is the ponderosa. This beautiful one hundred and eighty foot tree with its three or four foot diameter base is logged for lumber all over the Northwest, although it does not grow on the wet west side of the Cascades.

There are a few other softwoods or evergreens in the old-growth forest. The mountain hemlock is not typically logged as it grows at higher elevations. Likewise, the subalpine fir and subalpine larch are not the most sought after although the subalpine fir is used for lumber and pulp in some areas. The whitebark pine grows above forty-five hundred feet throughout the West but is most valuable as a wildlife tree. In fact, it is critical to a number of species including grizzly bears and the ubiquitous Clark's Nutcracker throughout the West. Dramatic losses due to white pine blister rust and mountain pine beetle have been seen in recent years. This being a non-commercial tree there has been a lack of funding to support research and treatment of these problems.

We must also note the Rocky Mountain juniper, found throughout the Northwest and used commercially for fence posts. Lastly, the madrona is a non-commercial tree found in rocky areas along the Northwest coastal areas in old-growth stands. This tree is unusual in that it is a broadleaf tree that is also an evergreen. Like the western larch, a tree that turns a beautiful yellow in the fall and then sheds it needles, they both ignore the generalizations of what constitutes the characteristics of hardwood vs. softwood. The madrona is a broad-leafed evergreen, and the larch is an evergreen that sheds its needles. Nature does not conform to our taxonomy in all cases.

As I look out my office window in downtown Seattle, watching the cars fill all lanes of the pavement, seeing the ferries cruise back and forth from the dock three blocks away, watching the near endless lines of buildings and houses as I drive home each evening, I am staggered by the amount of work it took to level all the giant fir and cedar that covered every square foot of this land two hundred years ago. How did they manage to do it?

As far as the rest of the country goes, there is the perception that this state is still filled with lots of wild places. Places where the same trees that were growing two centuries ago can still be visited. While there are not so many wild places as in the past, there is still some of that untouched land here. Look at all the roads and towns and cities and it is almost unimaginable that it has only been a touch more than two hundred years since Lewis and Clark paddled through just south of here.

It has always been about the Old-Growth Timber. It is so important I find myself wanting to capitalize the three words as though they are a proper name, a living being. It was the Old-Growth Timber that led to the troops of men in the mountains that finally resulted in the government setting aside large sections of land as Federal Forest Reserves that ultimately became the National Forest lands.

My first views of the timber left me stunned at the size and the numbers and the sheer volume of biomass that covered the land. I had much the same impression as that recorded by Vancouver and others. Centuries in the making but mere decades in the removal, the National Forests were under siege when I arrived in 1976. Many people were worried then about the dramatic loss of the resource. Today, the logging activity has dropped to a trickle compared to that time thirty-five years ago. We like to think we know more now, or that we are more enlightened and more sensitive about how we treat the land, and maybe that is true to some extent. But all this is still at risk. In spite of all the land set-asides and legislated protections, it is all still in peril, even more so from the subtle change of weather that means more or less rainfall and warmer or cooler temperatures. And now, more than ever from the intensifying fires that are upon us as a result of a hundred years of misguided fire management. What seemed like such a good idea, to stop fire from destroying the forest, has turned out to be the absolute wrong thing for us to have done.

In spite of the continuing loss of habitat, and in spite of the removal of millions and millions of trees over the past two hundred years, you can still get out and lose yourself in the wild places in the Cascades and Olympics. And you can still imagine what it must have been like all those years ago to be able to walk for miles and days on end and never actually see the sun, not because it was raining (although it may have been), but because you were buried in the enormity of the old-growth Northwest rain forest. Even today, in some places, you can experience the giant trees surrounding you on all sides for as far as you care to look.

It is true there is less acreage in old growth today. All the more reason to join in protecting what is left. However, before feeling overwhelmed by despair, visit the North Cascades National Park, or Mount Rainier or Olympic National Park. Drive to the mountains, enjoy the National Forests, and hike into the preserved wilderness areas. Much has been lost, but much has also been spared for us to enjoy and to pass to our children.

The old growth brought me here. It was the old growth that attracted the loggers and later resulted in the creation of the Forest Service. Things haven't really changed that much. It's still all about the timber.

Arrival

Ok – so what if I didn't exactly plan it out thoroughly? I did have at least a basic, although somewhat vague, idea of what it was I wanted to do with my life. Having already been introduced to the Northwest and the dramatic scenery of this country from earlier trips west, it seemed enough that I would go back to it after graduation from university. And so, I did.

Just out of school and without much in the way of financial resources, I found myself driving cross-country heading west in my very well used Corolla traveling toward the Cascades on Interstate 90 one June afternoon. In my possession was a letter from the Civil Service Commission, confirming my appointment to a position as a seasonal employee of the United States Forest Service on the Mt Baker-Snoqualmie National Forest.

Although most of my years had been spent elsewhere, it felt as if I were coming home as I followed the highway up the eastern slope of the mountains toward Snoqualmie Pass. This was the day I had been looking forward to the entire time since I had left the Northwest to go to college. It was, I believed, where I was meant to be. My parents apparently had no knowledge of this, having raised me halfway across the country, out of sight of anything like these mountains. But now, here I was, back in the rugged country of the Cascades.

I was going to work for the Forest Service, so what else could I be but a forest ranger? Thinking about it made me feel good. It sort of suited my desire to be somehow a bit different. Since I had never known anyone who was a forest ranger, it certainly felt as though that should be different. Also, since I had little idea what a forest ranger did, I was certain I would have experiences completely unlike any I had ever had before. In this frame of mind, I joyously watched as the trees grew bigger and the forest became thicker as I traveled deeper into the mountains. What kind of trees they were, I could not exactly say. Pines, I supposed. Some forest ranger I was.

Later that afternoon, having traveled over the mountain pass and down the other side, I stopped in a small Western Washington town and made the purchase of an alarm clock. I certainly didn't want to oversleep on my first day and I was tired from the long time I had been on the road. My new clock and I headed away from US Highway 2 and, following the roads shown on my map, I headed toward the town of Granite Falls, the last outpost of civilization before I reached my new duty station on the Monte Cristo Ranger District. I wondered at the name and where it came from.

From the small logging town of Granite Falls, the Mountain Loop Highway makes its way east along the valley of the South Fork of the Stillaguamish River, which is named for a tribe of Native Americans that settled the area long before it was defined as valuable timber country. It was a late spring day, a Sunday afternoon, the sun was shining and I was surrounded by dense stands of enormous trees. I could only see a short distance into the woods as I sped along since the trees and the brush were so thick. I had no idea what kinds of trees they were or why they grew so thickly or grew so impossibly huge. It did not occur to me to wonder what could possibly make the underbrush so dense. It was sunny and warm and I was excited to begin my chosen career. What more could there be? I would find out later about the rain.

I located the ranger station without problem since it was situated immediately alongside the road. Practically everything was located right alongside the road, when there was anything to be located, because the valley of the South Fork of the Stillaguamish is very narrow with steep sides that rise several thousand feet to both the north and south. As I stretched myself out of my car at the end of the long days of travel, I saw a beautiful mountain standing just to the south. It was only a few miles away and showed a sheer rock face that led to its summit. I could see a great deal of snow that extended well down the mountain. The highest elevations were still in full sun since at these northern latitudes, June days go well past 9 PM. I was finally at my new home.

Being a pleasant spring weekend, the information desk at the Ranger Station was still open and I met the first of the many people that I would come to know very well over the next years. Marie was a long-time resident of the valley and had been employed by the Forest Service for years. She directed me to the crew house farther back on the compound.

"Drive up the driveway and make the second left. You'll find the crew house at the end of that road."

All that remained was to show up for work in the morning, sign the usual pile of government paperwork, and I would be an official forest ranger. At least that was the image in my mind as I moved my few belongings into the empty crew house.

The First Day

The first thing the next morning, I hurried into the building having never met, talked to, or otherwise communicated with my new employers except by the non-discriminatory means of the U.S. Mail. I am certain they were just as unsure and just as surprised as I was. I cannot imagine taking a job now without meeting the people I would be working for and talking in great depth about not only the position but the organization; trying to get some sort of feel for what I was signing on for. To think of moving myself halfway across the country with only the promise of work from some letter - well, I guess the exuberance and adventurousness of youth enables us to do such things.

Having done so, however, I found myself employed by the United States Forest Service. And having gone through the requisite first day forms and paperwork, I was then off to get a tour of the district from my new boss.

Captain Pete was what we all called him. Not that first day, of course, but after I had been around a bit. I don't think it was ever to his face, but that is how we all referred to him that summer. Captain Pete was the supervising post-sale forester on the Monte Cristo Ranger District. He was my boss on my first job after graduating from Missouri State University with a degree in the fine art of managing wildlife. Of course, the specific discipline of wildlife biology was a small field that required considerable experience and time to enter into, so I had taken a job with the Forest Service thinking that by at least working for one of the government agencies that could potentially employ me in my selected field, I would increase my chances of finding such an opportunity. That is how I came to be a forest ranger. Actually, as I soon found out, what I became was a forestry technician, which is a very different thing from being a forest ranger and something else again from being a forester. In its simplest form, the forester is the officer. The forestry technician is the enlisted man. The forest ranger is the commanding officer of the base. That is the difference on the surface, and of course, the work itself is suited to the different roles.

I came from the Ozarks. Because of that, I had the impression I was familiar with rough ground - hills and cliffs and the like - and I suppose it might be true that when compared to say, a young man from Iowa, I was more likely to have experienced steep terrain. That first day, though, I don't think I was one bit more able to comprehend what I was seeing and doing than that fellow from the corn fields of Middle America.

It was not as if I had never seen mountains before. After all, hadn't I lived in Washington State for the years I spent in the Navy on Whidbey Island? Hadn't I been introduced to the Cascades and even done some hiking and backpacking then? Well, of course I had! And hadn't I driven several times from my ancestral home in Missouri across the Rocky Mountains and even crossed through the Sierra Nevada one time? I had seen the mountains. I had been there. My friend Roy had even brought his Montana climbing skills into my life and taught me to rock climb. So what was the problem? What was wrong with me? Why, when I looked down the slope alongside the logging road was I so unsettled? It was because I was expected to step off the road onto the steepest terrain I had ever considered trying to stand on without having a rope attached.

I was eager to impress my new boss with my knowledge and my skill and reinforce his decision to hire me. I did not yet understand the rules of the Civil Service selection process. I did not know at that time the explanation for why my name had floated to the top of a list of available candidates. Nor did I know that this left him with no choice but to offer me the position. If I said yes, he had to do the same. It was sort of a shotgun wedding kind of thing. That's how I came to be standing alongside the logging road, looking down the slope at a recent clear-cut and listening as Captain Pete talked about fuel loads and moisture content. And then he was gone. Over the edge. He was bounding down through the slash, which is the residue left after the loggers get what they want, and finally stopped some fifty feet below me.

"Fuel sticks." he said as he held up what looked like five small wooden dowels held together in a life raft fashion. The device was about six inches wide by eighteen inches long. He was weighing it on a small scale he produced out of his vest. I feared that if I stepped off the edge of the road onto that unbelievably steep slope, I would simply fall all the way to the bottom. That was about five hundred feet I guessed. And I might just take Captain Pete with me on the way down. At least when I had gone through that rock-climbing phase with Roy, I had been roped up in case of a fall.

"Oh well" I thought. If I didn't prove my worth to him now, I never would. Over the side I went.

Imagine standing on a hillside that is so steep you can reach out your hand and without bending over, touch the ground. Look the other way and all you see is air. How in the world could anyone slog through this mess while packing a chainsaw? How was it possible to cut and retrieve the enormous trees that had been growing on this hillside for hundreds of years? I simply could not fathom it.

"The fuel sticks absorb moisture and give us a sense of when it's dry enough to burn without being so dry that we catch the surrounding timber on fire," Captain Pete said, continuing his educational monologue while I carefully looked for solid ground on which to place my feet, dazed, confused and unsure of myself.

I guess the fuel sticks were not always right because a few weeks later, after I had acclimatized considerably, we burned that clear-cut. Actually, the term was "unit", as in "logging unit". We also burned up a considerable number of trees at the top of that insanely steep hill in the process, cooking to death several hundred old growth-fir and hemlock trees. That is the inexact detail of fire science. But then a lot of the crew was made up of people like me so it should have come as no surprise to anyone that the fire got away from us.

Captain Pete was from Sweden. He was just a few years older than I was but unlike me, he had not had to wish he could avoid going to

Vietnam by staying in school, or as in the case of some American lads, by going to Sweden. He had ridden the boat the other direction and come to the United States. He wanted to fly helicopters in Vietnam. And so he did. He continued to fly for the National Guard on weekends while he worked the forests of Washington. Captain Pete opened my eyes to a number of things, not only about the art of forestry and life in the Forest Service, but about people and opinions. He also gave me something that no other supervisor ever offered me while I worked for the agency - the complete freedom to succeed on my own. Thanks Captain Pete wherever you are.

By the end of the first day, I had been driven to only a small part of the district that was to be my home for the next two years. It took months to cover most of the roads and this was considered a small ranger district. By the end of that first summer, I had driven to the end of every road on the Monte Cristo Ranger District, hiked about three-quarters of all the trails, and wandered into areas that I felt certain had never been visited by humans. That was probably not true, but to me it felt that way. I was still a novice visitor to this country. I had experienced rain, snow, lighting, windstorms, floods, fires, bugs and bears, but nothing stands out quite so clearly from that period as that first day and my anxiety over the steepness of the ground.

I also learned the origin of the district name. Monte Cristo was one of the most well know mining towns in the state of Washington. It was located at the very east end of the valley in which the ranger station was sited. In the 1890s, it was believed that this area would be the greatest lead, gold and silver mining area in the Western Hemisphere. The name was inspired by the Alexander Dumas novel, *The Count of Monte Cristo*, and referred to his theme of regained fortune for its inspiration. With money backers such as John D. Rockefeller involved in the mining venture, there was high anticipation of fame and fortune. These optimistic hopes, unfortunately, did not materialize. It was a major mining location in the late 19th century but now is virtually gone. Today the Forest Service is undertaking a massive cleanup of the area to remove the toxic leftovers from the glittering days of a century ago.

Learning My Way

Over the next several weeks, I continued to learn my way around the station as well as around the district. The district compound centered around two buildings that fronted the highway, both of which had been constructed by WPA crews in the thirties. These public projects built by the Works Progress Administration and the Civilian Conservation Corp, were the result of public employment projects pushed through by Roosevelt's New Deal in 1935. The buildings were designed and constructed to adhere to the typically rugged and appealing architecture of that period. Pretty much any place you travel in the United States you will find such structures at many government sites that have been around since those days. They tend to be made of massive log beams and many big rocks. They look as if they will last a long time after we've gone.

The main office housed the visitor desk with its maps and photos and a few stuffed examples of the local wildlife. This was all most people ever saw of the Forest Service - the visitor information desk where they bought maps and asked directions to the trails and campgrounds. The Ranger's office was in this main building and from there Ranger Joel was the overseer of projects that could be loosely divided among his three principal assistants covering the areas of timber, recreation and fire.

In the same building was the district Resource Assistant or RA. If it had to do with anything except timber or fire suppression, it fell under the jurisdiction of the RA. That covered all manner of recreation, water, wildlife, grazing, mining, and huckleberry gathering, all of which were items under the direction of this position. Also in the same building was the office of the FMO or Fire Management Officer. This is a high profile area that is responsible for much of the image the public holds of what the Forest Service represents. Over time I learned that this was probably the least desirable district on the entire forest in which an FMO would pursue his craft since the average annual rainfall at the ranger station is over 130 inches. The beauty I remembered from my first drive up the Mountain Loop Highway and the impressions that were formed then were soon explained once I gained a realistic understanding of the temperate rain forest environment. Whereas most FMOs were charged with the always dangerous and usually difficult task of suppressing fires, on the Monte Cristo District, a good FMO was one who was able to light things on fire when even the gasoline and kerosene of a drip torch had a hard time maintaining combustion. It was that wet.

Out the back door of the main office was a covered breezeway, also built of great wooden beams and supported by rock and wood pillars, which led to a small house that had been converted to serve as home to the timber crews. Here was where the Timber Sale Officer, the TSO, and his staff operated. Although the Forest Service has always maintained that it pursues a multiple use policy under which the agency supports recreation, watershed management, wildlife habitat, and forestry, the undeniable truth of the matter is that it has always been driven by timber. Logging has been the heart and soul of the operation from its earliest days and in the mid-1970s, it had never been truer. Timber then was still king. At that time, it was very much the case that recreational aspects and fish and wildlife held distant spots behind logging and road building.

There were a few different groups holding court in the timber office on the Monte Cristo. The lines were drawn along road building activities, pre-sale work and post-sale tasks. The crews were divided according to those functions. Road building I assumed I understood although there are many details involved with scraping out a road sturdy enough to carry the weight of the logging equipment and trucks along the side of a cliff. Pre-sale involved everything up to and including the removal of the logs from the clear-cut. That meant they conducted initial surveys to identify likely locations for harvest, defined sale boundary layouts, and performed cruising to determine the actual timber stand contents. It also involved scoping out road locations and managing the timber sale bidding process and then overseeing the activity necessary to remove the trees. It was a huge operation when taken as a whole. Post-sale crews took over after the last log truck pulled out and were responsible for disposition of the debris left from the logging, replanting of the ground and then managing it up until the moment that it was ready for harvest a second time.

At the time I worked on this district, virtually all timber sales were still directed at old growth. These beautiful trees were all hundreds of years old. I was aware of only a few stands of second growth that were approaching harvestable age. I never saw any activity with second growth since there remained enough old-growth pockets to harvest.

There were some small sales as well, what were termed "salvage" sales usually resulting from blow downs. The blow downs were frequently caused by the original timber sale, which opened areas to wind exposure, thereby helping to create the salvage sales along the edge of the clear-cut, albeit unintentionally.

Also on the compound was the crew house, providing a home for a number of the seasonal employees. After I had arrived to find it empty, several more people moved in later to join me. There was the warehouse and garage and a gas house with pumps for fueling vehicles and saws as well as fuel storage for the drip torches used during slash burns. A small, refrigerated tree cooler shed provided a climate-controlled environment for the bags containing thousands of young tree seedlings that were planted every spring. Then there was a home for the Ranger and his family as well as a few humble houses that were used by the other permanent employees on the district.

Of all of the districts I have visited or worked on over the years, the Monte Cristo was the most pleasant. It was the architecture, the lovely, timbered location with the dramatic mountain views as a backdrop, and perhaps, the fact that it was my first station. I only know that typically I see ranger stations that are built of low cost government structures that are entirely functional but also very unappealing. Although relatively inexpensive and entirely practical, they usually sit in the midst of areas scraped clear of timber with the most likely views being that of the parking lot and highway. The Monte Cristo Ranger

District was different. Although administratively it has since been combined with a neighboring ranger district to the north, the buildings remain in use today as the Verlot Public Service Center and the site is just as lovely as ever.

The crews, mostly made up of seasonal workers, were divided along the same organizational lines as the front office. The Resource Assistant had crews that were responsible for all of the recreation activities. Campground maintenance required several people who made daily forays into the many campsites on the district. Their duties ranged from collection of fees at the pay sites to garbage pickup and picnic table construction. In addition, they were the most common public relations people on the district, often being called upon to provide directions, naturalist interpretation, settle disputes between neighboring campers and provide roadside assistance to stalled motorists. During these days, there were no campground hosts as we see now and most of the locations were first-come-first-served without fees. Funding for this work came from the general revenues the Forest Service generated from timber sales. Also on this team were the backcountry rangers, who spent their time hiking the miles of trails. They provided information for needed maintenance on the trails as well as served as the naturalists for those hikers they encountered. They were also involved in what seemed a great many lost and injured hiker rescues over the course of the summer. The recreation crew was the group that delivered the Forest Service experience for the majority of visitors.

Fisheries and wildlife each had a small contingent tasked with collecting and maintaining information on the animal life and watersheds of the district. Every timber sale and road building project involved these people who provided environmental impact information as the fisheries team attempted to mitigate damage to non-timber resources during the logging cycle. This was the kind of work I had hoped for when I hired on, but as I learned, these jobs were exceptionally difficult to land.

The FMO, the Fire Management Officer, had a crew of ten firefighters on hand. Since things were typically so wet, there was not a lot of local action seen by this crew. From time to time, they would be dispatched to lend support on fires that were on other districts and other forests, most usually on the dry, eastside Cascade forests. When on duty on the Monte Cristo, they stayed in shape physically by being the crew that provided needed maintenance to those trails identified by the backcountry rangers as requiring attention. In addition, they were locally known as the BD crew, or Brush Disposal crew, and would perform such burns as were necessary to clean out the residual debris from logging - the "slash" - when such burns could actually be accomplished. Actually, the slash burning exercises involved pretty much every hand on the district with the BD crew being the heart of the team. Everyone had a chance to work at dealing with fire.

Being a member of the Forest Service was somewhat similar to my stint on aircraft carriers while in the Navy in that everyone was a firefighter. In both cases, it is easy to justify this. At sea, if things start burning, you'd better be a part of the suppression team since there is no such thing as dialing 911 and waiting for the fire engines to arrive. The same holds true on a ranger district. When things start blazing, everyone grabs a shovel or Pulaski and goes to work.

While these teams were maintaining the campgrounds and trails, the pre-sale crew would be crawling through the brush and timber, fighting their way through the thorny devil's club, locating and managing the primary resource on the forest - the trees. Pre-sale foresters would locate likely stands for harvest and determine how and where to site roads, define the boundaries of the sale, mark the boundaries and then survey the timber by "cruising".

Cruising is a skill acquired through apprenticeship and much practice. A skilled cruiser can provide information that will determine the grade and quantity of the timber that will be removed from the sale site. The numbers provided serve as the basis for loggers to make bids for removing the trees, agreeing to pay a certain amount based upon the content of the stand. Pre-sale personnel also worked as sale administrators and were on site while the logging was taking place. This ensured that any regulations designed to keep streams clean or roads open were followed. They also verified that only those trees intended for harvest were taken, by painting the designated boundaries of trees to be removed with a bright colored strip that would be visible both on the removed trunk and on the remaining stump.

During the first summer of my employment, I watched with fascination as the loggers arrived with their collection of equipment.

There were huge metallic contraptions that all seemed to need paint, dripping great pools of oil and hydraulic fluid on the landings, which were the wide-spot-in-the-road areas where the equipment was positioned. Great steel towers were erected at most of these sites and were guyed with thick steel cable. These cables stretched in all directions and were attached to tree trunks to provide stability for the tower. More cable ran into the clear-cuts from the top of these towers with cleverly designed hooks called "chokers" that enabled the cables to be wrapped around a log. The grinding and rumbling machinery at the base of the tower then dragged the "choked" log uphill to the landing. A bit less environmentally damaging was the so-called "high-lead" logging that held one end of the massive old-growth logs suspended in the air, only dragging the tail portion uphill, leaving fan shaped trails radiating from the tower into every corner of the clear-cut. These are visible when one views the clear-cut from a distance. By keeping the log suspended from one end, damage to the underlying ground was lessened and interference with the uphill travel was reduced.

For particularly sensitive areas, a type of removal was prescribed in which the logs were pulled completely above the ground and transferred to the waiting landing without touching the ground. This technique, called suspension logging or skyline logging, involved stringing cables completely across a valley. In one case that I observed on the district that first summer, a good mile of cable stretched from one side of the Coal Creek valley to the other. The choker was attached to this massive suspended cable and was reeled out until the entire supporting cable would be slackened enough so that the choker would reach the ground. Once there, the choker-setter, the person in undoubtedly the most dangerous position on the hillside, would wrap the choker cable around the log, secure it, and then move away to get clear. The suspension cable would be reeled in until the entire log would be pulled into the air. Suspended in this fashion, the massive tree trunk would be pulled in mid-air back to the landing. Imagine the stresses and weight involved with this. For me, the marvel at watching this operation never grew old. Although I was working at this point in the post-sale part of the logging operation, I frequently stopped to watch the show while I was out in the field. In the mid-1970s with the amount of timber that was being removed from the National Forests, there were always many of these shows to watch.

I had long been a hiker and a backpacker. From my earliest exposure to the mountains of Washington, I had taken every opportunity to travel the trails and see the sights. Over the years, my collection of gear necessary to support such activity and make it somewhat comfortable had grown. The backpacks of the time were still largely aluminum frames with external nylon bags. I had a nice gas stove, a good sleeping bag and a sturdy pair of boots. The boots were what I planned to use in my new work. Being full grain leather with Vibram lug soles, they provided both support and protection. They were principally designed to be used when carrying loads and traveling on trails. It didn't occur to me that when pressed into service for my new career, they would be of no more use than a pair of sneakers.

The essential problem was one of traction. When traveling on a graded trail the rubber lug soles provided good grip and the sturdy leather uppers offered the needed support and security. However, once I stepped off the trail or road into the natural terrain of the Pacific Northwest, I would have been better off barefoot. Fairly quickly I traded the ankle high boots for a pair of ten-inch tops, although still with a lug sole, in an attempt to avoid some of the problems that I immediately encountered in off-trail travel. When I was moving slowly and cautiously, it was possible to select my path in such a manner as to avoid most of the slipping and sliding. At least it was that way when it was dry. The problem was it was very rarely dry. The basic issue of traction was not solved even after spending seventy-five dollars on the new lug sole work boots. I was hard pressed to squeeze my four-dollar an hour salary to buy another pair. I endured being on my face and butt so much that later that summer I finally did break down and buy the first of what would turn out to be many pairs of truly functional boots.

"Corks" was what we all called them. Technically, they are caulk boots. They work because sticking out of the sole are several dozen short little spikes – caulks - and along the edges are steel hobnails. With these boots you can climb along downed logs and, providing the bark does not peel off underneath you, walk with carefree speed and a moderate sense of security. Once I laced these mid-calf high boots on, I was able to markedly increase my ability to travel in the rough terrain. Add to the corks a pair of baggy "Can't Bust 'Em" jeans supported by a pair of suspenders and a heavy, cotton gray and white striped "hickory" shirt and I became indistinguishable from the real loggers. As a crowning mark, I cut the sewn hem from the bottom of my jeans so if the material became snagged on a branch or on the brush, it would easily tear away. This was more than just to assume the look of the "high-water" logger's pants. When working around the incredibly hazardous machinery and saws, more than one logger's life was spared when he was able to pull free from some snagging item. Leaving the rolled and sewn hem in the cuff could easily have made the difference in being able to rip free before the swinging cable or escaped log could strike you down. My friend, Vern, used to tell me what it took to do this work.

"You've got to be pretty light on your feet to set chokers". Being able to move quickly required both the traction of the corks and the non-snagging "breakaway" pant cuffs, and to some degree, a gymnast's agility.

There was other equipment that was necessary to round out the well-dressed woods worker look. Of primary importance in this climate was rain gear. Most everyone wore the same kind, made of a heavy rubber-coated nylon that usually came in only one color, dark green. Once in a while, someone would show up in yellow. Although yellow seemed to make sense from a visibility standpoint, for some reason none of the "real" loggers would wear anything but green. It was simply not part of the uniform. Inside this waterproof garb, you could be guaranteed that no rain would leak in, except around the collar. It would have worked very well if one simply stepped out of the truck and stood perfectly still along the edge of the road. What really happened, however, was that as soon as you would begin to move and work, the moisture released by your body could find no way through the entirely waterproof fabric. This was long before Gore-Tex was invented, but it would have never been used in any event simply because the breathable modern fabrics would not last more than a few days when subjected to the kind of abuse that was common in this line of work. The end result was that the raingear replaced a soaking by precipitation with a soaking by perspiration. The one big advantage was that it was always warm inside the impenetrable gear, even if it was damp in there.

The other thing that was indispensable to this career was a good lunch box and thermos. These days I still tend to pack my lunch with me to work, but I use a nice nylon, insulated bag. Such a container, if thrown in the back of a pickup and bounced around with tools and boots and gas cans, would have resulted in having nothing recognizable left by lunchtime. The same problem was rapidly made clear for the coffee that I carried in my thermos. The standard glass-lined thermos I brought with me didn't last through the first day. It was replaced, as was the paper lunch sack, with steel containers. My Stanley thermos is still with me to this day and although it's beat-up, scratched and dented on every surface, it still keeps a few cups of coffee warm. My lunch box is a similarly battered tool that sits in my garage now. From time to time, I would paint it some wildly loud color to cover the latest rust and dents. Its last coat was a very bright fuchsia that clashes horribly with the baby blue color that I applied to my metal hard-hat but at least that made them both easy to find.

All of this official outdoor gear was hauled about in one of the U.S. Forest Service vehicles that we uniformly referred to as "green-rigs". A "rig" was defined as any vehicle that was driven into the woods, unless by a certain type of independent logger, known as a "gyppo", who rode around in "crummies". So let me clarify. A truck used by an independent logger was actually a "rig" but was always referred to as a crummy. A truck driven by a Forest Service employee was a "green-rig", so called because it was painted that unmistakable pale green used universally in the woods at the time. I have noted that these days, all trucks operated by the Forest Service are painted white. Probably because they are all leased, again unlike the past, and the generic color makes it easier for the leasing company to resell. I miss the symbolic "green-rigs".

Donnie B. was one of those mechanically minded individuals who somehow seemed able to diagnose and fix any problem you presented to him. He was in charge of the warehouse on the district and in that capacity he performed all the maintenance on the district's vehicles and equipment. At times, the damage we inflicted during the course of our work exceeded the capabilities of the tools at his disposal and he would be forced to transport the broken part or vehicle into town to a shop, but most of the time we'd just limp into the warehouse with something dangling or dragging or allow him to listen to the noises the truck or tool made and then leave it in his hands. He also took care of all of the small equipment that included chain saws and pumps and a hardware store variety of hand tools.

The only task that he allowed us to perform routinely was to gas and wash the vehicles. These were items that were not considered options. Each day we were required to fill the gas tank, check for the more obvious issues under the hood, keep a detailed log of where we went and how many miles we drove and report any and all discrepancies immediately. Every Friday we were responsible for cleaning the rig that was assigned to us. These were the routine chores around the station, and like taking out the garbage, they were done every time without fail.

The warehouse was also the site of a few other things in addition to maintenance. It had a large meeting room upstairs over the garage that served as an assembly area for various training activities and as the site of the annual "step test". The step test utilized a box about eighteen inches high that a prospective firefighter would step onto and then back down to the floor repeatedly for a period of two minutes or so. This elemental exercise, performed long enough to get the heart pumping pretty hard, provided a very crude means of determining how fit the candidate was by measuring the length of time necessary for the heart rate to recover from such exercise. Certain guidelines were established for anyone interested in working a fire. If your step test recovery rate was outside these parameters, you were considered unfit to perform the incredibly arduous work required when on a fire line.

For the people who wanted this work because it carried with it the double benefit of hazard pay and overtime, failing was bitter news. On the other hand, many people disliked the fire work and the conditions under which it was performed so badly that to them the misfortune came if they managed to pass the test. Today the step test has been replaced by something known as the "pack test" in which an individual is required to carry a 45-pound loaded pack over a three mile course in a time of forty-five minutes or less. This new approach is probably a better measure of one's fitness for the work involved in fire-fighting, but as crude as it was, the step test managed to weed out those who were not in top condition.

Even for those who failed the step test, escaping involvement with fire was difficult and at times impossible. The Forest Service routinely conducted slash burns, which they usually referred to as controlled burns although more often than not they were anything but controlled. Their purpose was to clear the debris left from the logging activity. Imagine, if you can, what it is like to ignite twenty or more acres of rather dry firewood. Of course, it does not all go up at once. At least it usually does not.

In Western Washington, the amount of rainfall received had a tendency to make slash burns problematic. In addition to getting permission from the state Department of Ecology to release the high volume of particulate matter, planning involved finding a time when there was a period of dry weather to allow the slash to reach a state where it would ignite. Many times, attempted slash burns remained just that – attempted slash burns – because the debris was simply too wet to catch fire. Further complicating the matter, ignition timing was always intended to light the fires just ahead of an incoming weather system in hopes of using a good soaking of rain to help put things to rest once the cleanup was accomplished and to take advantage of westerly winds to keep the smoke out of the populated Puget Sound lowlands. Overall, the FMO spent a good deal of time planning, arranging and hoping, only to see the anticipated burns be followed by delays and even cancellation. In spite of all the hindrances, sometimes we would actually get things to light and the entire district would turn out in an effort to control the big burn. Sometimes all the planning and preparation actually paid off. This was the case on the very first slash burn in which I was involved.

Rotary Creek

During my very early days with the Forest Service, I was introduced to the concept of the slash burn. This event is intended to rid the landscape of the debris left behind by the loggers after they had extracted everything they deemed valuable. The remainder, consisting of limbs and tops, broken and shattered logs, the undesirable chunks from a size or species perspective, all of these were termed "slash". I find it interesting to note that during the 1970s and 1980s when I was working in the woods, loggers often extracted cedar logs that been left lying on the ground after having been cut around the turn of the century, the 1900s, by the old-timers who found them too massive to drag out with the tools of the time. I recall one timber sale in particular where the most valuable wood on the sale was not the standing hemlock and fir but the downed cedar logs that had been lying for seventy years underneath it. Even now, we are beginning to see our earlier logging practices as unnecessarily wasteful. One hundred years ago, only the very best cedar was taken out. The other trees, if they weren't needed for mining timbers or railroad ties, were simply left where they were cut in order to get them out of the way so the cedar could be extracted. Our contemporary practice of burning the leavings will no doubt be viewed as just as wasteful by the much more resource stingy thinking of the future. In some countries, the left over slash is already being utilized for both commercial power generation and as ground cover used during the logging operations to reduce site damage. But in 1976, we just set it on fire.

Forgetting for the time being the likely error of our ways and merely accepting fact as fact, let us return to the disposition of the slash that was left behind. Scientific forestry at the time preached that the only good clear-cut was one that had been cleaned and sanitized so the reforestation effort could proceed unimpeded by debris and leavings and, particularly in the Northwest, the residual mistletoe infestations that were commonly found among the old growth. This is not your Christmas time "kissing-under-the-mistletoe" variety but a relative that, like all parasitic mistletoe species, infects a host and draws its sustenance from it. This plant, officially known as dwarf mistletoe (*Arceuthobium spp.*) has long been considered a pest since it inhibits the growth of the big trees. In yet another irony of nature, it turns out that recent studies have determined this plant to be a keystone species, meaning it affects many other organisms in a way that far exceeds its relative biomass. Most ironic is the role it plays in nesting for the Spotted Owl, the current most popular indicator of forest health throughout the Northwest.

The mistletoe that infects the big timber of the Pacific Northwest is found in many tree species. I have never seen it in cedar or in any of the hardwoods, but the commercially more valuable fir and hemlock species suffer significantly from loss of growth caused by the strength-sapping effects of mistletoe. To a forester, this was always viewed as being akin to boll weevils in cotton or grasshoppers in the wheat fields. A very effective deterrent to the continued spread of the parasite is to reduce an area of infestation to carbon. This tends to remove any residual elements of the parasite from the immediate area and forces it to invade from neighboring, infected old-growth areas, assuming there is any remaining old growth. In any event, this slows the spread of the parasite. The process at the time was to dig a fire line around the perimeter of the clear-cut in order to have some definition of control, and to have a place for the fire crews to stand, and then light the entire thing on fire. This was, as bizarre as it may sound, a positively delightful experience.

My introduction to slash burning took place in an area known as Rotary Creek, located along the northwest slopes of Mt. Pilchuck, a far west pioneer mountain that extends as deeply into the Puget Sound lowlands as is permitted in this mountain chain. This is the same lovely mountain, visible from the parking lot in front of the Monte Cristo Ranger Station, that greeted me on my first day. There were a couple of things about this particular "unit", as the clear-cuts were referred to, that were fortunate for me, the novice slash burner. First, it was relatively small. It covered only about twelve or fifteen acres as I recall. Secondly, it was nearly level. At least, it was level in the relative sense of the term as far as ground found in this part of the world. Size and slope are significant since lighting a slash fire consists of starting at the high point of the unit and making cross slope traverses with a drip torch.

The drip torch is a metal can that contains a bit more than a gallon of a mix of gasoline and diesel that is "dripped" through a foot long, spiraling metal tube that culminates with a nozzle containing a fiberglass wick, which has been set alight. The amount of fuel fed to this wick is greater than the wick can absorb so the excess is leaked out, ignited as it passes through the burning nozzle, and "drips" onto the ground. The gasoline gives the necessary volatility and the diesel prevents instantaneous explosive ignition. The "glop" that falls on the ground, or more likely on the slash, burns long enough and hot enough to ignite whatever object it contacts. Typically, three to five people will make a pass across the slope, each somewhat behind and below the person ahead. Spacing between these individuals determines just how much slash will be set on fire at a time, thus controlling to some degree, the size and enthusiasm of the blaze. The process of beginning at the top of a hill makes sense when you envision the results of subsequent passes across the hill at lower and lower elevations. The heat from the fire tends to pull the burn toward the top of the hill. One of the fascinating aspects of fire is its singular ability, among elemental components of earth to defy the laws of gravity. Starting at the top means that by the time (in theory) you reach the bottom of the area, the upper portions have had time to burn most of the residue clear, thus providing an ever widening fire line against the top of the clear-cut, which typically provides protection to whatever timber lies uphill from the conflagration.

Even though the Rotary Creek fire was relatively small and, as I mentioned, relatively flat, a great amount of time was expended in preparation for igniting the remaining slash. Not only had many hours been consumed in building the hand line around the perimeter, but several days before the event, the district fire crew had started positioning hoses, pumps and hand tools and planning for delivery of as much water as possible. This included setting up a portable water tank, in this case the Fol-da-tank, which is rather like a square version of the back yard above ground swimming pool. This was filled by a combination of tanker truck delivery and pumping from nearby streams. After all of this preparation and approval from the air quality folks at the state, and after the careful development of a plan and a thorough review by all parties, the big day arrived.

On the morning of the lighting of the Rotary Creek slash fire, everyone, it seemed, knew every move. As the procession of Forest Service "green rigs" made their way up the gravel road to the scene, the event began to unfold like a well-rehearsed play. The district fire crew was the earliest to arrive and they had laid out several hundred feet of one and one-half inch hose along the road that bisected the unit, as well as a length or two up and down the fire lines on each side. This provided a reasonably complete coverage of the timber along both sides. This hose lay stretched not all the way to the top or to the bottom, but about halfway. As the crews arrived, trucks were positioned at safe locations, yellow Nomex fire shirts were slipped on over t-shirts, hard hats were donned and water bottles were attached via web belts so that each worker could remain fairly independent. Everyone knew exactly what their job was, what their position was to be, and how to proceed. Everyone, that is, except me.

As the new guy, I was dispatched to attend to relatively minor tasks. Presumably, I would do things that were useful but not critical and certainly not dangerous. I was also assigned to the watchful eye of an experienced crew-member who could serve both to demonstrate what to do and when to do it, but could also keep an eye on me to prevent me from creating a problem of any kind or finding a way to injure myself or others. Essentially, my task this first day was one of observation. Watch how the job is done. Watch what people do. Listen to the radio chatter. Perhaps then, I could be of some real use the next time.

Once the drip torch crew began work and ignition progressed gradually down the slope, I did in fact begin to get more of the picture and from time to time would do something of value, such as throw a few shovels full of dirt on a spot fire that had crept outside of one of the side lines and begun burning in the adjacent timber. These events were never allowed to become more than minor episodes but still, I had the chance to participate.

As the final few passes were made along the very bottom part of the unit, the crew had become somewhat jammed up in the lower reaches of the area since the top portion, above the road, was more or less burned out. By then it was midafternoon and all parties were growing weary and were eager to move ignition along at a pace that would allow sending most of the crew home after a reasonable day. This was caused not so much by the kind nature of the management on the district, but the very real need to conserve finances and avoid paying overtime for crews when it was not essential. That money needed to be held on to in case of real fires, the wildfires not the controlled burns, and the need to fund the suppression efforts for them. This budgetary emphasis caused the drip torch crew to be moved at a considerably faster pace than had taken place up to this point. With the increased number of people available to staff the fire lines and with the top two-thirds already burned clear of slash this was a sound decision on the part of the District Ranger and the Fire Management Officer, who were immediately responsible for such activities.

Things heated up in a real hurry as the rate of ignition was increased and in almost the time it takes to tell it, the slash was burning very hot and fires began to spot on the outside of the line where I was working. Being on the downwind side, we were subjected to both the drift of the smoke and the flying embers that were causing these spot fires. Within a few minutes, everyone assigned to my side was busy. The call went out for half of the crew from the opposite side to move over and reinforce in order to prevent a real fire from starting in the old growth that bordered the unit. As the radio call was made for these people, the District Ranger walked up to where my mentor and I were busy throwing dirt at a burning fir tree. We had at this point dropped below the end of the lowest hose that had been placed along the fire line.

"Willard, hustle up to the road and bring down two lengths of the black rubber hose," he barked at me and then without pausing for breath he instructed my partner to get connectors and attach the hose that I would be bringing to the end of the inch and one-half that ended a short distance above where we stood. Things were beginning to get interesting. This being my very first experience with fire in the woods, I had no idea if this was routine, unusual or an impending disaster. I assumed in my enthusiasm that it was the latter. I raced away, moving as quickly up the incline as I could, trying to remember where I had seen the fire crew stack the hose that I was charged with retrieving.

Finding it once I hit the road turned out to be no problem and I grabbed two coiled bundles, threw one over each shoulder and turned back down the hill. The hose coils were one hundred foot lengths of heavy-duty one inch rubber garden hose. It is the same kind you have hanging on the side of your house, maybe just a bit sturdier. Together, taken with the task of climbing down the hill along the hand dug fire line, they were a load and I was panting and sweating by the time I reached the end of the inch and one-half run. Standing there was the Ranger, my partner with the necessary hardware already attached to the bigger hose and several others, ready to use the water on the ever-growing fires outside the line. I felt like I had done a fine job and had impressed the Ranger with the speed of my return until I looked at him, noticed that he wasn't smiling and heard him say,

"Uncoil them."

That was all. No smile. No "well done". A flat stare, a sense of error, and for me, complete surprise. With my emotions in total confusion and having no clue what I had done wrong, I dropped both coils to the ground and kneeled to being untangling the hose. As I removed the proper end for my partner to connect to the larger hose, he looked at me and said,

"You should have uncoiled them on the road and drug them down the hill, male end in your hand. We'll play hell trying to untangle them down here." No one, of course, had mentioned a thing about that in the confusion and the rush to get water to the fire. He was right. It took a good fifteen minutes to unroll and stretch the very stiff rubber hoses down the slope, made the more difficult by the twisting, stump and brush filled terrain. Several times during this exercise, I saw the Ranger looking at me. His expression told me that he had clearly identified me as a complete bumbling city-bred idiot and he would make certain to keep an eye on me in the future. I do not think he was impressed.

In spite of my mistake, the fire was eventually controlled and only a few of the trees outside the line were scorched. The water from my late arriving hoses was useful but all parties indicated to me that the results would probably have been the same even without it. This did nothing to soothe my bruised ego. From that day on, I asked questions when I didn't understand, moved as fast as I could up and down the hill, threw more dirt than anyone who stood near me, and in general, tried every way I could to redeem myself in front of the Ranger. Whether I succeeded or not I cannot say. He never told me.

The First Summer

So it was that first summer I began to learn about the cycle of life in the woods. There was the natural cycle, of course, of spring rain and the lengthy daylight hours of summer. Some of the days were hot and some of them dry, but most often it was another weather system rolling through bringing more moisture and reawakening the bugs. The long days of summer in this northern latitude and the abundant rainfall were the keys to life in these mountains. The temperate rain forest climate and the good lowland soils along the river bottoms were the perfect habitat for growing the huge fir and cedar that the loggers wanted so badly. The timber industry was only replying to the demand for wood. I began to understand how it's not fair to blame the logging community for the loss of the old-growth forest in this country. Although they are the ones who take most of the blame from the environmental organizations, it is the consumer public that has ravaged the landscape. It's always easier to blame the group doing the extraction than to admit to ourselves that the demand for construction and growth and the generation of wealth is the real driver and that we have to accept responsibility ourselves.

Even that first summer I began to experience the conflict between diverse ideas of harvesting and of preserving the forest. I know now that we have unfairly charged the cutters of the trees with being shortsighted. I live in a house framed with Douglas-fir and clad with beveled cedar siding. On all four sides of my house are decks - nearly twelve hundred square feet of them and all made of cedar planking that is attached to a fir and hemlock structure. All of the window casings in my house are clad in cedar, most of the floor is oak, and all of the doors are wood as are the kitchen cabinets. Mine is not the only wood house in the neighborhood. I was beginning to see the problem even that first summer. I still have personal conflict over the ideas of harvesting and preservation. On the one hand, it's sad to see the utter devastation of a clear-cut. On the other, it's hard to see the economic devastation on the small communities that depended on timber for the welfare of the town. This conflict continues today over all resource extractive industries. I still waver from one view to the other and while I understand both perspectives, I cannot offer a solution. It is clear, however, we need to be seeking some sort of balance in our approach to managing this resource.

Pick any point in the cycle of scientific forestry and begin there. It could be at the initial planning stages of a timber sale, or at the time of replanting a logged over unit or at the time of the slash burn, or even at the moment of germination of the seed that has dropped into the duff underneath a mature tree. It matters less at what point we start than it does that we consider the entire cycle. As long as people inhabit the earth, and as long as we have not succeeded in removing every available stick of wood, (something which has happened in a number of places already), we will continue to swarm over the landscape and log the timber. As I began to understand that first year, the best we can do is to try and think about what we are doing, and attempt to replace most of what we are losing.

After the cut and after the burn, what remains is a land of stumps and brush. At times the slash fires are so hot that all of the organic matter that has collected on the surface of the ground for decades is incinerated, leaving a sterile mineral base. Rarely, however, are entire areas cleared to such an extent and usually there remains a layer of duff and litter and debris to protect the soil to some extent. The next step in the cycle is to replant the area that has been logged.

It was this replanting activity that gave me the greatest sense of relief as I watched truck after truck loaded with logs driving down the Mountain Loop Highway heading for the mills in the lowlands. The thought of replacing what we had removed met with a degree of approval in my environmentally concerned mind.

There is no point in denying it. The focus was always on the timber. When the federal government first sent its rangers into the wilds of the Northern Rockies, the mission was to protect the timber. It is true that by protecting the timber you also protect the watershed and the wildlife. The real point in protection has always been to make it available for later removal.

Logging is a lot like fishing. It involves going face to face with the barest aspects of nature and it means doing it in whatever conditions may be presented. Both of these occupations continue to be fraught with danger.

Winter

In early November of that year, the first skiffs of snow fell on the peaks towering above the valley. Termination dust we called it. Starting in September, as the pace of work slowed, the seasonal crew was slowly reduced and people had begun to drift back to whatever occupied their lives through the months of the year when they didn't work for the Forest Service. Many of them were students who used the seasonal work as a means to earn tuition money for the coming school year. On the other side of the desk, some were teachers who also returned to the classroom. Others spent their winters working as ski lift attendants or ski patrol at the slopes both locally and around the country. From time to time, one of the more ambitious of us would manage to find winter seasonal employment with agencies that provided better winter weather in places like Arizona and Florida and sometimes in Texas. For many of us, including me, the upcoming reality of termination was a time of uncertainty. I had already begun working to try and understand the Civil Service hiring system so that I could become a permanent employee and not have to deal with being out of work every time the snows came.

By the end of November, we were reduced to the occasional foray up the Mountain Loop Highway to burn a roadside brush pile that had been collected from some summer project. With the ground covered in snow, it was safe to pour the kerosene and gasoline mixture on these piles and light them. A crew of two was adequate since no additional help would be required because there was virtually no possibility of the fire getting away from us. It was more likely we would spend an entire day unsuccessfully trying to get one of these brush piles lit. There were also the routine end of season tasks of putting tools away, making sure that all of the shovels and Pulaskis and hoedads were sharpened and the shining edges painted to prevent rust. Chain saws would be cleaned and overhauled. All of the green rigs would be cleaned up and in some cases parked for the winter. There were also a few trucks that had been around all summer that were cleaned and driven back to the dealers from which they were leased. By the time all of this was done, and the few remaining inside paperwork tasks were completed, there remained no further reason for the district to retain my services. I had reached the end of my first season.

Rivers, Railroads, Roadways

Since the end of the last ice age, somewhere around fifteen thousand years ago, the trees of the Northwest and the Cascades have sprouted from seed, grown to maturity and then died. These trees existed in a world that included only the most elemental of intrusions – wind, water and fire, and the occasional volcanic eruption. Nothing else much touched the lives of these quiet giants. Until man.

When humans first arrived on the scene, even they had essentially no impact. The trees were too big, too massive to handle and there were just so many of them compared to the number of people that any attempt on the part of humans in intercede in the quiet life of the trees would have simply gone largely unnoticed. Those early days of human interaction with the forests were only a tiny blip on the massive screen of life that occupied a scale so out of proportion to the human population as to be unnoticeable. Even with the early inhabitants of the Northwest cutting trees for canoes and lodges and sometimes setting things on fire to clear land, the impact could be largely discounted simply because of the relative scales between the two groups – the people and the trees.

By the early 1800s, this began to change. Lewis and Clark drifted down the Columbia in 1805. After them came a flood of settlers and adventurers. By 1810, Canadian fur trappers had a fort built in the Spokane area. In early 1825 Hudson's Bay Company built Fort

Vancouver and the influx of people came even more rapidly. At that same site, the first sawmill in the Northwest was built, the earliest beginnings of what became a major industry.

The sheer number of human inhabitants along with the mind-set of these people and the tools they brought with them began to make it possible for them to challenge the enormity of the Northwest forests. The first efforts at cutting took place immediately along the saltwater shoreline, with the trees dropped alongside or directly into the waters of Puget Sound. And why not? There were so many trees and they were easy to get at. Cutting them and getting them directly into the water meant they could be easily handled, relocated and taken to where they were needed for building piers and ships, the massive logs becoming masts and keels and even planted vertically in the water to support the docks of what would become the seafront cities of Seattle and Tacoma and others.

It started slowly at first, with only axes and the time and energy it took to hack laboriously through the up to twelve foot thick trunks of cedar and fir. Gradually the shoreline timber disappeared and horses and oxen were used to drag the logs from farther inland to the waterfront along "skid roads". The logging moved away from the saltwater shores to the rivers where once again the timber could be dropped directly into the water of the flowing streams and guided downriver to the waters of Puget Sound. Soon these riverfronts were depleted of timber and animals were again pressed into service to drag the logs from farther and farther away to the river banks.

The event that fueled most of the timber cutting in the Northwest took place in California. In 1848, when gold was discovered and the "rush" for wealth began the following year, a huge demand for timber was immediately created. Getting the easily accessible timber from the Northwest was simpler, it turns out, than trying to cut and transport from the geographically closer Sierra Nevada. Transport by water from the Northwest was faster than overland hauling. As a result, the California Gold Rush became the timber rush for settlers and loggers in the Northwest. Soon money from California investors poured into the Northwest and mills began to spring up all along Puget Sound and the Columbia River. At the time there were no laws governing the cutting and removal of timber, thus making the resource free for the taking, allowing great fortunes to be made and encouraging completely unregulated logging.

In 1850, the Donation Land Claim Act was enacted by Congress, offering 320 acres to anyone willing to make the trip to Oregon Territory. The population continued to increase and the resultant pressure on forest resources grew in step with the new settlers. As these folks arrived, timber was cut to provide housing and to clear land for farms. A subsequent congressional bill, The Homestead Act, provided the same access to free land as did the Donation Land Claim Act, but opened up areas outside the Oregon Territory to settlement with the same pressures when those areas were located in timbered country. But even with the influx of population and the increased logging activity that followed with the California gold rush, there was still a limit to just how much timber could be cut since all the work still needed to be managed by hand tools and livestock in order to move the trees to market. That changed in 1881.

In that year young John Dolbeer from New Hampshire was looking for a way to realize his dream of striking it rich in the post-gold rush days of California. He had gone to the gold fields in 1850 and began building lumber mills to process the timber that was initially being shipped from Oregon and Washington. In 1881 he filed for a patent on his steam powered logging engine, the forerunner of all of today's mechanized devices for dragging trees out of the woods. This machine revolutionized logging overnight. No longer were animals needed to move the logs from where they were cut to a central location. And not only did this engine replace the use of livestock, the machine could outperform them. By the mid-1880s, the steam engines were in use on rivers in the forests of Washington. Around the same time, the ax, which had always been the standard gear for falling these great trees, was supplemented by the big crosscut saws. Trees could be felled and moved much faster now. Still not satisfied, the inventors continued to add new technology. It was in the early days of the twentieth century that the first gasoline powered chain saws appeared. Although a far cry from the tools in use today, this further increased the speed with which loggers were able to get trees on the ground and was one more step in increasing the total number of logs removed.

As the new century got under and the timber continued to recede with the old growth being found farther and farther away from the water, new ways were being explored to move the logs to market. In spite of the growing expense and difficulty in getting at the timber, logging continued to be the dominant industry in the Northwest. The short line railroad spurs that had been laid up many stream beds were soon connected to feeder lines that allowed transport of the logs by rail rather than by water, thus allowing even greater control of the work and increasing the industrialization of the logging industry. Mills no longer had to be situated along water to pick up the downstream log traffic, although many still were, but could be built anywhere so long as they could connect with the railroads. By 1905, Washington was the number one timber producer in the entire country, with one billion board feet cut that year.

By 1913, trucks were being employed to transport logs. When World War I broke out the demand for the high quality Sitka Spruce exploded in response to the need for light structural wood for airplanes. The U.S. Army assigned troops to build roads to allow better access to the trees and trucks became the dominant form of transport as the volume of timber removal continued to increase. Following the war, the road network continued to expand and surplus army trucks appeared everywhere with a dramatic increase in the number of log hauling enterprises.

By the 1920s there were many gasoline powered saws in use and the first motor vehicles appeared that were sturdy enough to begin replacing the hauling capacity of the railroads. The use of trucks was far cheaper than a railroad and road construction continued to boom. The early roads were puncheon or cross-plank covered – logs laid crosswise across the cleared area to form a wooden surface for the trucks to travel. Building these roads was slow work, labor intensive but still far cheaper than a railroad and used materials found on site rather than having to import the heavy steel for rails. Eventually the puncheon road was replaced with the easier to build and cheaper gravel surfaced road, also a product of improved vehicles and tools. One of the biggest impacts of these advances was that the ability to use trucks allowed smaller operators to enter the logging business since building a railroad was a massive and expensive undertaking, and something only available to those with the economic power of a corporation behind them. More logging operators translated into more and more roads and more and more logging. The cycle of expansion continued as a seemingly endless stream of small operators entered the increasingly accessible market. By 1926, the harvest had expanded to 7.6 billion board feet per year. This remains the historical high mark for logging in Washington.

With the spiraling increase in activity, the forests began to show the negative signs of this massive harvest. Because of the density of trees in these Pacific Coast forests, it was often decided that clear-cutting was the optimal harvest technique. It was hard to drop one tree without hitting one if its neighbors and damaging it, so the conclusion was that the adjacent tree might as well come too. Then it would hit the tree next to it – and so on. What was left behind were thousands of miles of roads leading from one clear-cut area to another. Much of the land in private hands in Western Washington was simply cut to the ground, leaving hundreds and eventually tens of thousands of acres of stumps and nothing more. At the time there was no effort to reforest any of this since the supply of additional timber seemed limitless. Regrowth was left up to nature and the natural distribution of seed. This natural reproduction grew more difficult to achieve as the clear-cut areas continued to expand in size. Unfortunately, by just looking toward the horizon, the loggers would see hill after hill of uncut, old growth just waiting for them to push the road an additional few miles. And so they did.

As the number of miles of roads increased and the number of incursions into the Forest Service land increased, the federal agency created a department devoted solely to the management of roads. The road engineers connected their operations with the timber sale process creating a situation where the logging company bidding on a timber sale was also going to be in the business of building the access roads. This at least gave the oversight to the government rather than to the private contractor bent on extracting every tree in sight. This also put maintenance of the roads in the hands of the Forest Service so that once a timber sale was completed the access into the area remained. This was a boost for access in firefighting as well as recreation, making areas accessible for hikers and hunters that had previously been simply too remote to easily get to. This also turns out to have been a mixed blessing.

In the end, today the Forest Service in Washington manages some 22,000 miles of roads in the various National Forests of the state. That compares to 175,000 miles of total roadway in the state. That includes the interstate freeways, federal and state highways as well as city streets. That's a lot of roadway for the cash-strapped agency to take care of. Other states in the Northwest exhibit similar numbers.

It has changed over time. The Forest Service is not a well-funded agency any longer. This is caused both by the massive decrease in logging on their managed lands and resultant decline of revenue – there is simply not that much old growth left – as well as the financial insolvency of most federal agencies in our current economy. There are few new roads being built. There are many more that are being gated and left to return gradually to the wild. It will take many years, but even now, many of these gated roads are filling with stands of alder, these pioneering trees making a first attempt at reclaiming the space. In addition, there are many miles of road that are intended to remain open for fire or recreation access, but that are closed by damage. Years of neglect and flood erosion to surfaces and washed out bridges has resulted in miles of roadway being inaccessible, as the money for repairs simply does not exist.

Perhaps it's all part of the cycle. For multiple reasons, the massive logging and road building craze of the post-World War II logging era has been replaced by a more thoughtful and conservative time, caused both by a more balanced approach to our need to be stewards of the land, and what may ultimately be the good fortune of bad economic times. The lack of funding very well may be the breath needed by our beleaguered forestlands. It may provide a chance for them to recover from the onslaught of axes and saws and chainsaws and the intrusion of railroads and puncheon roads and gravel roads. Maybe now is the time to let those pioneering alder trees break up the surface of those now abandoned roadbeds and make way for the return of the giants.

The Learning Continues

The New Year found me living deep in the mountains. It was the first time in my life I had spent a winter in such country. I was still fascinated by just about every aspect of the experience at that time and I found myself strangely relaxed and enjoying the feeling of near hibernation that accompanied the incessant rain and snow and cloudy weather.

Days didn't really begin much before eight. The valley of the South Fork of the Stillaguamish is very narrow with steep ridges lining both sides of the westward flowing river. Since November, the days had started late and ended early since the sun never managed to penetrate to the valley floor even on those rare days when it appeared. I was in the shadow of the ridges until March. Actually I don't remember if the sun ever did break through. I have very strong memories of waking every day to rain and going to bed every night, still to rain. From time to time, it cooled down enough that we would get a bit of snow. Never too much fell since we were at less than one thousand feet in elevation and only a few miles from the ocean. Although my home was deep in the mountains, the weather was still very much moderated by the not too distant waters of Puget Sound.

I spent those days living on the eastern side of Mount Pilchuck, the western sentry of the Cascade Range that served as the rain catcher for the weather systems that blew down from the Gulf of Alaska. As the unsettled, wet air was forced up along the slopes of the mountain, the moisture was squeezed out of the clouds to fall on my roof when I was in the house, and on me, personally when I was not inside. And for a lot of that winter, I wasn't.

Since being laid off for the season from the Forest Service, I had spent much of my time waiting for the next work opportunity. I was not yet completely broke, so I enjoyed the slow pace and for the first time in my life, I actually stopped moving long enough to read and write and play music in the leisurely fashion I had enjoyed as a youth. The years of going to school days and working nights had left me exhausted and frenzied. At the same time, my marriage of eight years had ended abruptly the prior summer when my wife appeared at the door and announced that we needed to end our relationship. Dealing with that, and the sudden change from the fast pace of my earlier life meant that the quiet time was much needed and much appreciated.

By January, I had prepared to go to work on a tree planting crew for Scott Paper Company near the small town of Granite Falls. Scott Paper was the major private landowner in the area at the time and because the government mandated that clear-cut areas be replanted, they employed several of us to help them meet the legal requirements. Many years later Scott sold off all of their holdings and simply departed the area, but that was after they had removed every single bit of the old-growth timber on their land. It is obvious now that the replanting was in no way intended to provide an ongoing source of wood, but merely to ensure the ability to continue mining the old-growth resource until there was none left. Scott Paper did not seem to subscribe to the idea of a renewable resource that many companies emphasize in their operations.

It is sometimes hard to get young trees to grow in many areas of this country. While that may seem difficult to believe, keep in mind there is only a short time frame in which to accomplish the work and there are many ways to plant the trees incorrectly. After the small tree seedlings are in the ground, they are completely on their own. Unlike your garden, where you water, fertilize, and spray for pests, the tree seedlings are left to live or die based upon the quality of the stock of the seedlings and the chance occurrences of weather as well as the quality of the planting. Water being the most immediate need, the planting tends to be most successful if done as early in the year as possible, but after the presence of and danger of more snow has passed. Since the majority of land owned by Scott was low elevation at under 2000 feet, we were able to begin work much earlier in the year than was the Forest Service. So in February, the planting season was underway.

Work began at six-thirty. In Washington in mid-winter, six-thirty is dark. It was usually still near dark by the time we had loaded up our bags of trees and tools and driven in the crummy to the job site. As soon as we arrived, it was out of the truck and into the corks and rain gear and then start swinging the hoedad.

The trees were bundled in brown craft paper bags with a moisture proof liner. The bags are about the size of a hay bale and each held several hundred seedlings depending on their size. From the time they were lifted from the beds at the nursery, they were kept in these cellophane-lined bags and stored in temperature and humidity regulated rooms in order to prevent growth prior to being put in the ground. This ensured that whatever food reserves were in the roots would be available once the tree was introduced to its new home.

From the transport bags, the trees were placed in individual portable planting bags that were worn around the waist. These bags were insulated to provide additional protection during the planting process. Each planter would stuff as many trees as could be safely carried into the bag since many times we would be quite a distance from the road and the truck and resupplying could be a problem. The usual planting tool was a long handled shovel called a "hoedad" with the blade turned at a ninety degree angle from the handle so that it could be held in one hand and swung, plunging the nearly two foot long blade into the ground. By swinging with one hand and reaching into the bag for a tree with the other, we were able to make rapid progress across the clear-cut areas. When the ground was covered with brush or litter or the organic layer found in forests, called duff, the hoedad could be reversed or turned sideways and a short, sharpened blade could be used to scrape and cut, or the long, flat side could be used to help clear away debris. This enabled us to reach mineral soil - a necessity for the tree to survive.

The first time or two swinging the hoedad gives one little indication of just how incredibly fatiguing this process could become. Clad in wool socks and long underwear, the cutoff jeans held up by suspenders that were worn over the usual blue-striped 'hickory' shirt and, most days, shrouded in the non-breathable rubber rain gear, we swung those 'dads from first light until day began to fade around four pm. Cold and wet and fatigue do not begin to describe the conditions. The first day I thought I would die. The second day I hoped I would die. By the end of the first week, I began to have fears that I would not die and that I would be doing this forever. After a month, it felt as if I had always worked this hard. The strength in my arms and back seemed to be tenfold what it had been before I began the work. As a crew, we no longer complained but began to tally the total number of trees that we had planted individually each day. It became a contest to see who could put the most in the ground. Sixteen hundred a day became the norm for each of us - about four acres.

In spite of the seeming mindlessness and brutality of this work, it was surprisingly enjoyable. I'm sure that must seem hard to imagine, considering that we were always cold, tired and wet. My boots didn't really dry even on the weekends and by nine in the morning my socks would squish when I walked. Being continually wet and buried in mud, my hands, even though they were gloved, became as dry and rough as brick. By day's end, every part of my body ached as we continually drove ourselves to higher and higher numbers. Despite that, the work was satisfying in a way that I rarely experience today as I work in an office. Knowing that every tree had to be put in the ground correctly or it would die meant that even as we raced across the clear-cut units, we planted each one individually and with care. Being able to turn around at the end of the day and survey the physical dimensions of the area that I had planted gave me a very real sense of worth. Today, all these years later, I still sometimes go back to those areas that I planted.

When I look at trees that are over one hundred feet tall, I know that what I did was worthwhile.

Eventually, the work ended as the days became longer and warmer. By April, it was time to call a halt to planting in the lowlands and bid farewell to my employment as an industrial tree planter. Before they let the planting crew go, however, the company wanted some help with one rather exciting adventure.

We had planted a large tract of land located adjacent to the Tulalip Reservation, near the popular Tulalip Casino located just inland from the coast on Northern Puget Sound. When we finished the several hundred acres of replanting, there were plans to burn large areas of nearby land that had recently been logged. This was another parcel of almost two hundred acres that Scott Paper owned and from which the old growth and some second growth had just been harvested. As was typical, the ground was cluttered with piles of tops and branches and the usual slash leftover from logging. The land was nearly flat and was surrounded on three sides by more timber, which was not all owned by the company, and on the third side by our just replanted acreage.

Unlike the Forest Service, the industrial forestry company took a big-picture view of things and subscribed to the theory that using a bigger hammer would get the work done faster. So rather than lining up the twenty of us with drip torches and letting us light this monster a bit at a time, a helicopter showed up.

While I was asking the rest of the crew and our supervisor what was going on, and none of us really knew, I saw a large flatbed truck arrive with a collection of fifty-five gallon steel drums onboard. They drove up to the landing where the helicopter was parked, loosed a hoist from the side of the truck and started loading barrels onto the helicopter. The contents of those barrels, it turns out, was the kerosene-gasoline mix used in drip torches. To enliven things further, the helicopter crew produced a giant-sized drip torch nozzle and mounted it on the side of the chopper.

I was aghast at what I was seeing. Clearly, the helicopter was going to fly over this large clear-cut and pour burning gasoline on the litter below. Then they took off, and did just that.

Twenty of us on the ground with hand tools and a couple of pumps that we hadn't bothered to test run were completely inadequate for what ensued. Wasting no time, the boys on the chopper had at least one hundred acres on fire within twenty minutes. It was the biggest burn I ever witnessed in my life. It exploded into a boiling cloud of black and grey and white smoke and towering flames a hundred feet high. We scrambled for the nearest line of timber and frantically dug and chopped and tossed dirt as we tried to prevent it from slopping over the lines. With the addition of more help frantically rushed from other job sites, we managed to hold things to a minor disaster, only losing a few acres of someone else's timber. Fortunately, there were no houses in the area at the time. A very long day of heat and smoke and endless struggle and we had managed to burn the entire unit down to dirt. Other than actual wildfires, I never saw anything like it again.

After the early season ended with Scott Paper, I took my new, high speed tree planting skill and marched back to the Forest Service at

Monte Cristo where I had been rehired to begin my next season of adventure. This year the first day check-in held no surprise for me and I felt much more comfortable arriving for the coming summer than I had the prior year. I met with Captain Pete, who was still running the pre-sale crew and who had selected me to return for another year and discussed plans for the upcoming summer. It should have been no surprise to me that the first task on the agenda when I arrived there was, of course, tree planting.

Stocking Surveys and Stand Exams

I was into my second pair of cork boots. The beating taken by a pair of boots, when they were always wet and used on steep and rocky terrain, meant they wore out quickly. After finishing the spring planting on the Monte Cristo Ranger District, and after having worked several months at Scott Paper for their more generous wages, I was a bit more wealthy than I had been in the past and I was able to secure a high quality pair of boots for the first time. Walking into the district office that second season, well-oiled Buffalo brand cork boots hanging over my shoulder as I readied for work, I no longer felt like the rookie I had been just one short year earlier. Now I was able to offer advice and training to the new crop of seasonals that soon came on board, impressing them with my knowledge and experience and demonstrating my sure-footedness as we explored the steep terrain of the district.

I had learned by this time about more than how to plant trees and was conducting reforestation stocking surveys, which were performed on recently replanted clear-cuts. Having by now planted tens of thousands of trees, I considered myself something of an expert on the care and feeding of these juvenile trees and spent many days with one of my new cohorts conducting counting surveys of the reforested units. It was really all about making sure that a reasonable number of trees were surviving and that the mandated reforestation of logged areas was successful. In some cases, replanting was needed to cover losses caused by weather, or from poor initial planting or from animal damage. Deer, in particular, loved to browse on the tender young trees. To counter this, many times the seedlings were treated with a chemical – Thiram – to deter deer. Thiram is a sulfur based fungicide that also makes the treated plant unappealing to deer. As you might suspect, continuous exposure to this chemical can cause any number of unpleasant reactions. Of course, this was never mentioned to us when we planted, probably because no one bothered to mention it to our supervisors. In any case, the deer knew enough to stay away from it. That's more than I can say for those of us planting with it. It turned out that due largely to complaints from tree planters' continued exposure, rules were enacted to regulate the use of the chemical and in many cases, it has been discontinued.

After working extensively at completing reforestation stocking surveys I eventually graduated to performing exams of older trees. Initially it was in units that were in the fifteen-year age range with specimens the size of good, healthy Christmas trees. Of course, by the time they were this age, things were unpleasantly crowded since the planted four hundred trees per acre norm (about one tree every ten feet) meant that there was no space between branches. In addition to the replanted stock there were usually some natural seed trees growing as well. It also always seemed to be wet when we needed to survey a stand of this age. It was like walking through a car wash.

When the trees reached this age, the district forester would usually prescribe a pre-commercial thinning if the stand looked healthy. Meant to offer a bit more growing space for individual trees, this procedure involved sending a crew with chainsaws into the thicket and cutting some number of them down to provide for more rapid growth for the remainder. It was when I learned this it became clear to me that we were farming. We planted more trees than we expected to survive and cared for them until they were so thick they needed to be thinned. Thinning the young trees was exactly like thinning a patch of radishes.

From time to time, I would get lucky, have a stand exam in an older collection, and actually get to see trees that were mature or nearly so. It was in these stands I saw the real giants. These were the trees that were hundreds and hundreds of years old and many feet thick at the base. This work in the old growth soon became my favorite and over the course of my career, I did more of this than any other kind. My final years were spent in the old growth, doing these same sorts of surveys, able to be with the giants of the woods.

Change of Command

It was mid-summer of that second season when Captain Pete announced he was accepting a new posting on the Forks Ranger District of the Olympic National Forest. For a true timber rat, this area was the Holy Grail of Forestry since they still pulled bigger timber out of the Olympics than anywhere else. Some of the Oregon National Forests may have had a larger total cut at the time, meaning more board feet were removed than on the Olympic, but in terms of big trees, there is just no place like the Olympic Peninsula. For Captain Pete it was a great opportunity to pursue his career. As it turned out, it was also a great opportunity for me.

His leaving also coincided with the departure of his second-in-command who had decided he wanted to return to more familiar, and flatter, terrain as he also resigned his post and moved back to his home state of Texas to work for their state forestry department there. Surprisingly, that left me, in just my second season, as the senior member of the post-sale forestry crew. Just three seasonals and me who each had an average total experience of six weeks.

I was still working as a forestry technician, and my pay remained a generous four dollars an hour, but suddenly I was solely responsible for carrying out all the duties formerly handled by Pete and his assistant forester. Without allowing anyone to notice my nervousness, I jumped enthusiastically into the opportunity and took charge of the crew of seasonals for the rest of the year. It was a bit of a stretch given I had only slightly more experience in the field than they did, but I wanted to seize this opportunity as I still had visions of landing that permanent biologist's job somewhere down the road.

This change of command also allowed me to learn some new things. For starters, I was exposed to the Forest Service's data collection and repository system that existed in the pre-computer days, and I learned my way around the Total Resource Inventory or TRI system. On this collection of large-scale aerial photos and Mylar overlays, our team recorded everything about our district that related to the work we did in the timber. Stocking survey info, stand exam info, prescription info for logging and reforestation, and the details for prescribed fire – it contained it all. I imagine it would appear primitive to anyone seeing it today, but it was quite impressive for the time. It required continual manual updates but served its purpose well, providing a centralized location for all of the collected management and planning data. As the year progressed, I learned more and more about entering and interpreting the data. This activity ended up keeping me working late into the year.

I was also thrust quite suddenly into the world of contract administration. We had a number of contracts for tree planting and pre-commercial thinning that were ready to start or were already underway when Pete left. This work still needed to be monitored, inspections needed to be made, contractual paperwork needed to be managed, and I had to figure all this out with virtually no assistance. There was a significant learning curve, as I needed to learn not only the specific requirements related to the contract paperwork and record keeping, but also to figure out how one went about physically inspecting the work that was being done. I also learned that although the variations between individual contracts were not great, each contract crew required its own special set of communication skills based on the work they were doing and how well they were doing it. Additionally I found myself involved with people from the forest headquarters office in Seattle for the first time, as well as having to deal with other government agencies. We managed, as a team, to stumble along, learning as we went and continued to make progress. As far as interactions with other organizations, it was during this period that I met the gentlemen from one state agency that left me with an unforgettable memory.

Poachers

"Dennis Willard report to the office," blasted from the primitive intercom connecting the main office building to the warehouse. While somewhat clunky by today's standards, this hard-wired system enabled two-way communication in an era long before telephone switching systems became commonplace and inexpensive. You pushed a button and talked over a wire. It worked well and had worked for years. I answered the call and said I was on my way to respond to the summons.

We were having a first-aid training session in the warehouse. The entire district was attending, with the exception of one or two people left in the front office. We needed to learn things like how to repair broken bones and plug large, gaping wounds caused by a fall in the steep terrain we explored. There were other things that might be useful as well, such as treating heat exhaustion, insect bites, and in this climate, foot rot.

It was in the midst of this training, when over the intercom, Marie from the front office made the announcement asking for me. Everyone turned and looked at me. I was just as puzzled as they were as to what was going on. On the way to the office as I was imaging all sorts of things, it finally occurred to me that I might know what was happening. It was something I had been somewhat anticipating for some time now and as usually happens with such things, it came when I was least expecting it.

Over the past several weeks, in my capacity as the government administrator on a pre-commercial thinning contract, I had become involved with the Washington State Department of Game. We had a group of thinners working on the district who were Russian immigrants now living in Oregon after having slipped out of the Soviet Union to China, then on to Africa then to South America and ultimately to the United States. This somewhat meandering route enabled them to avoid the difficulties of arriving in the U.S. as Russians, something not acceptable at the time. Instead, they arrived from Chile, Argentina, or a country that had a more lenient immigration standard from the U.S. Government.

For some time the Game Department had suspected that these individuals were guilty of illegal hunting. The state officials had, in the past, come to me to ask questions regarding the location of the camp where the thinners lived, of their activity in the area, and of anything I might have observed that would indicate illegal activity. At the time, I had no idea of how or why Fish and Game was on the trail of these men, only that something was up. With these recollections running through my mind, I entered the main office at the Monte Cristo Ranger Station.

No sooner had I walked through the door than I found myself surrounded by four of the biggest guys I had ever seen. They seemed to all be in the mid-six foot range and each was armed with a sidearm on web gear that also contained all of the usual police accoutrements such as handcuffs, flashlights and radios as well as other equipment I did not recognize.

"Where are they today?" they all seemed to ask at once. Trapped within this mass of intimidating law enforcement and not being a big guy myself, I was swept by a wave of tension inside that bordered on fear. I hadn't even done anything and these guys scared me.

"I'd make a terrible criminal," I thought to myself. As I began to explain the location of the thinner's camp, it occurred to me that the job of game warden is probably best dealt with by large and well-armed men. Consider the assignment they carry out.

Word arrives that someone is illegally taking deer or elk or possibly bear. Maybe it's duck and geese, but in all cases that individual is carrying a weapon. There is also the fact that this person is most likely knowingly breaking the law. When a firearm is involved there is automatically a serious risk to the law enforcement agents, but imagine the environment in this case - miles from anywhere, otherwise there would be no wildlife, and no one around to witness what is going on. That is the premise on which poaching is based. Somehow in this situation, big bodies and heavily armed seems to make sense. I'm thinking that the Department of Fisheries sounds a bit less hazardous, although I suppose the alleged perpetrator could whip you silly with their fly rod, or snag your ear on fishing lure and reel you into submission. Still, that is better than facing a big bore elk rifle.

After some discussion, the Fish and Game fellows finally asked me to lead them to the campsite. Following me in my favorite Forest Service green rig, I lead them up the 318 road to the sight of the camp on Canyon Creek, about forty-five minutes from the ranger station. There was no one at the camp since it was the middle of the day. The game wardens poked around the camp tent, dug in the fire pit, and wandered all around the area looking for some sort of evidence. While all of this was happening, I began asking questions trying to find out specifically what was going on.

It seems that over the past couple of years there had been groups of thinners from the same small community in Oregon who were traveling around the National Forests of the Northwest doing mostly pre-commercial thinning. It was brutally hard work and the pay was never very much, although for new arrivals in the U.S. who had limited skills and limited knowledge of English, it was a very good opportunity to become established while performing a valuable and necessary service. For whatever reason they chose to disregard, or did not understand, the laws governing the taking of fish and game. As a result, they would supplement their pantries with whatever fish they could catch, and as many as they could catch. They also tended to shoot whatever deer happened to present themselves.

Fish and Game had learned of this quite by accident when a Washington State Trooper had made a routine traffic stop of a pickup truck carrying two of these men home after the completion of a contract in the central Cascades. In the back of the truck were several fifty-five gallon barrels packed full of venison. This led to a full scale investigation of many thinning contracts with the department tracking down several groups of poachers, including the group I was monitoring at the time.

Over the next week, the thinning crew finished their contract for the Forest Service while the game agents quietly monitored the activity. The thinners did a fine job on the work, and shortly after I signed the final inspection papers, they broke camp, loaded their belongings into their two pickups and drove down the gravel road to the state highway where they were met by the four men who had accompanied me to the camp. A collection of other law enforcement officers was also in attendance. The thinning crew disappeared after that and I never again heard of or met any of that group.

Summer Doldrums

After surviving the pursuit of poachers, life settled down a bit for me and on the district. I learned during this period about the existence of negative reports. I still recall the day I was contacted by the Mt. Baker Forest Office in Seattle asking about some specific report that was due the previous week. My response of having no activity in that particular area was met with disbelief that I had not filed a negative report. Nothing to report means filing a report to report nothing. While I understand the reasoning behind this, it still makes me laugh.

During the mid-summer months, we tried to burn two recently logged units. The Bear Lake timber sale was located in a flat area along the eastern side of Mt. Pilchuck that held several small lakes. There were a few sales that had been conducted earlier in the year and although they were small, they still required the usual clean up. This sale was in what is probably the wettest location on the entire district as the slope of Mt Pilchuck is the first uplift encountered by incoming weather systems and the water is squeezed out of the clouds as the climb up the steep west face of the peak. Given that, a slash burn in that area was even more of a challenge than usual. As often happened on this district, the planned fire never happened, the fire refusing to catch. After several hours of pouring gas and diesel on the slash, we abandoned the plan to burn the area. All we really managed to accomplish for several days of preparatory work was to spend a lot of time and generate a lot of unpleasant smoke. The outcome was a mess of partially burned brush.

Not long after that, we mounted an attack on another logged area on Olo Mountain. We had even less success there in spite of weeks of preparation. Much energy was expended in building fire line, laying hose, setting up portable tanks with pumps and in the end, once again, nothing.

For several weeks, life settled into a quiet and comfortable routine. Days were the same – one after the other – riding the gravel roads to another reforestation stocking survey, or inspecting a thinning crew. It seemed to rain a lot with one weather system after another drifting in from the west.

In spite of the perpetual wet making slash burns a challenge, things were not always so damp for all locations in the district. At one point in that summer we had a spell of cooperative weather and managed to get about a twenty acre clear-cut for a sale known as Double Eagle to catch. This was a very memorable fire for me.

The Double Eagle Burn

As I gained experience and established some credibility with others on the district, I had moved up in the pecking order to the point that I was allowed to carry a drip torch as part of the slash burn lighting crew. As I mentioned before, the drip torch is a metal can that contains about a gallon and a quarter of a gasoline and diesel fuel mix that is dripped to the ground through a foot long spiraling metal tube that culminates with a fiberglass wick which has been set alight. The amount of fuel fed to this wick is greater than the wick can absorb so the excess is leaked out and ignited as it passes through the burning nozzle and then drips onto the ground. The mix of gasoline and diesel helps control the volatility and serves to prevent explosive ignition. Mixtures of from one part gasoline to one part diesel up to one part gasoline to four parts diesel allow the fire managers to control the volatility of the mix, thereby assisting in controlling the speed of ignition of the fuel to be burned.

Unlike other, failed attempts at starting prescribed burns over the course of the summer, this event had the right combinations of being preceded by a lengthy dry spell, high temperatures and low humidity. We were going to have no trouble getting this unit to burn.

The terrain for this timber sale was steep, with a road at the top of the cut area. In the middle of the unit the road expanded at its end into a large landing where the logging equipment had been positioned, allowing the loggers to high lead the logs uphill where they were limbed and bucked into appropriate lengths for transport on log trucks. The landing always ended up as a collection site for both the tops and limbs from trees pulled up, as well as containing a large pile of undesirable log pieces that were not suitable for market. Some of these leftover pieces were a result of breakage, with logs that were split or rotten. Much of this abandoned slash would end up as firewood as private woodcutters would visit the sites of recent logging activity to collect wood for the coming winter. This landing had quite an impressive collection of debris collected both on the edges of the landing and over the sides. All of this was contained in large, if somewhat unstable piles.

We started our burn out at the top, as was typical. There were five of us with drip torches making horizontal traverses from one side of the clear-cut to the other. As the newest guy on this crew, I was last, allowing me to watch the others and pick up pointers for how to best get things ignited. With each pass, the crew would stop, one by one, on the far edge and wait for all of us to make the trip across. The crew leader would then gauge the fire we had just started and based on how things were proceeding would determine when it was appropriate to make another pass. That way we managed to keep the fire hot enough to clear out the debris, but not allow it either to get too active or to cool too much. Things proceeded according to plan throughout the day and by mid-afternoon, we were starting on our last pass across the bottom of the unit.

This lower part of the logged area had a large rocky scree slope in the middle. About one third of the bottom traverse would be done through this rock after lighting the slash on the near side. As the last person in line, my crewmates were all on the other side and standing on the fire line as I entered the rocky area.

I was carefully picking my way through the loose rock and boulders, cautiously hanging onto my still burning drip torch while I made sure of where I placed my feet in order to avoid stumbling. I became aware of yelling as I was about mid-way across. It took me a moment to figure out that the shouting was from my crewmates standing on the far fire line. I stopped picking my way through the rocks and looked up at them to see that they were all shouting and waving at the same time. I could not quite make out the words since I was still just a bit too far away, but they were all energetically pointing uphill and waving frantically.

I looked up toward where they pointed. Careening downhill, directly at me was one of the large logs that had been left on the landing. It was big. And it was on fire, leaving a trail of smoke and sparks as it crashed and bounced my direction. It took another moment for me to comprehend what it was I was looking at. The log continued to aim directly at me, making lots of noise now. At some point in what had turned into a slow motion view of the world, I realized I needed to move or this two-foot diameter, twenty-foot long, tree trunk was going to take me down.

Somewhere in my brain, I unconsciously determined I needed to retreat in order to escape. I don't remember being aware of making a decision, but I turned, dropped my drip torch and made ready to run back the direction I had come from. In that instant of turning, however, I lost my footing in the rocks and fell hard on my back. And at what seemed the same moment in which I crashed painfully onto the rocks, the log passed over me in front of my face. I could feel the heat as I saw its dark bulk miss me by the barest of inches.

From the other side of the clear-cut, my crew mates saw me go down at the same instant the log passed over me. Later they said all of them were certain I'd been hit. They were equally certain I was dead. While remaining inert on the ground, on my back, I assessed myself, to ensure I was not, in fact, deceased. In a bit of shock, I simply lay still on the ground. Taking some time to check for pain points, I confirmed that all my limbs were attached and could be moved and that I was unaware of any blood escaping anywhere. In fact, other than being bruised on the back from crashing onto the rocks, I was unhurt. I was a bit surprised my mustache had not been burned off.

I was still looking straight up into the sky when I saw four faces over me, all looking very anxious. I must have grinned at them because suddenly they were all talking at once. It was as if I had returned from the dead. In truth, I was remarkably lucky not to *be* dead.

That was not quite the end of fire season that year. Just over a week later, I was working in the east end of the district when I received a call from the station. It seemed a recent lightning storm had started several fires in the vicinity of Glacier Peak, deep in the mountains to the east of our district. Jumpers from the North Cascades Smoke

Jumper Base in Winthrop had been dropped into an area adjacent to our district boundary. Over a couple of days, they had suppressed the lightning fire and were making their way out to the end of the nearest road. I was to pick them up.

Smoke Jumpers

Most people will make the immediate connection between wild land firefighting and the Forest Service. I did the same when I first began working for the agency. After all, I had seen Richard Widmark in the old movie "Red Skies Over Montana" when I was a kid. I learned from that film just how tough a guy it took to be a firefighter, let alone become a smokejumper. Now *that* was a career choice I could relate to, although I never really considered it a possibility, not for a minute. I still remember the first time I ever met a smokejumper. Actually, I remember the day I met four of them.

It was a late August day in my second year with the Forest Service. I was still working on the Monte Cristo Ranger District and had established a certain freedom after both of my supervisors left for other jobs. In their absence, I was left in charge and was effectively without a boss. This allowed me the luxury of choosing which things I would do and which things the rest of the crew would be responsible for completing. On this day I had chosen to travel to the far east end of the district and was enjoying the spectacular scenery.

I was working alone doing reforestation stocking surveys, essentially counting tree seedlings in recently planted areas, on the day the radio call came to pick up a group of jumpers that were finished working a fire they had attacked on the fringes of the Glacier Peak

Wilderness. It was during this period that the government had just begun to implement "let-burn" policies in which naturally caused fires were left alone so long as they ranged only through wild areas. When the fire entered what was deemed commercially valuable timber on harvestable land, the troops were dispatched. This was the case on this fire. Lightning had started this fire in the Glacier Peak Wilderness Area some days before and it had been allowed to burn naturally, with no interference, until it reached the Wilderness boundary. As soon as the aerial spotters reported harvestable timber going up in flames, a plane from Winthrop was dispatched and four jumpers arrived on the scene within less than two hours.

After they had managed to turn the fire back on itself and succeeded in putting it out, they needed a ride home. After a check of the maps, it was clear that the nearest road was only a few miles southwest, so they began walking. I was to meet them.

I got the radio call at lunch. I was sitting within earshot of the truck and happened to have the set turned on. In order to reach their takeout point I would have to end my project and make a roundabout trip to make it to the next ridge north of me. After having made the drive, I sat there for about an hour with no sign of anyone, just enjoyed the sun and the birds, and imagined what other jobs there might be in the world that would allow for such an experience as I was then having. A warm day, it was easily in the eighties that afternoon, and sitting in the shade alongside the road with a small stream flowing by was a perfect way to spend a summer afternoon. The only thing I could have imagined that would make it better would be to have been fishing in the stream that ran just below the road where I sat.

I heard them long before I saw them. At first, it was just a suggestion of voices. Coming and going on the wind so uncertainly that for a while I wasn't sure it was actually human voices but the mysterious sound one often encounters in the woods. A combination of wind and moving trees and water that gets all stirred around in the air and bounces from hilltop to hilltop. Too soft a sound to actually echo and yet it somehow manages to catch on the wind like dandelion fluff and travel great distances. You believe you can hear distant voices but it is just the wind playing this mysterious trick.

After a while, it was clear the jumpers were making their way out of the woods high on the ridge above me as the voices became discernible. I saw them as they left the timber and began making their way downhill through the clear-cut above me. Four men finally stepped out of the brush and onto the road just behind the truck. As they neared the road level, the noise they made had gradually increased, not just as a result of being nearer to me, but also, I think, for my benefit. Their arrival occasioned a lot of loud talk with yelling, joking, grunting and such carrying on. They dropped their large backpacks on the road and then climbed into the crew-cab pickup clearly expecting me to heft their gear into the truck bed.

As I look back, the thing I remember being struck by the surprisingly average size of these men. As I struggled to heft their carelessly dropped packs into the truck, I was even more impressed. The packs were large duffel bags with backpack straps and waistbands much like a conventional hikers pack. They were stuffed to overflowing with the gear they had jumped in with on the fire. Out of the jump airplane came all the tools and gear they would need for not only firefighting, but also food and shelter. Sticking out of the tops of two of the packs were shovel handles and chain saws. Inside, I knew, were their parachutes and protective clothing as well as all of the tools that had been needed on the fire. Axes, Pulaskis, hand saws, gas, oil. I suspect the packs each went somewhat over one hundred pounds and these people had just lugged them over several miles of very steep and rugged country without even the benefit of a trail. That's why the size of these guys got my attention. They were no bigger than I was. They were just one hell of a lot stronger and tougher.

The ride back to the Ranger Station was great fun as the four jumpers took turns telling me tales that may have been complete truth or complete lies. I do not know. After a number of years of working in this environment and of having known a few more of these people, I tend to think my skepticism may have been unjust. Some of the experiences of these jumpers are simply too fantastic to need any kind of exaggeration. I still recall the faces of these four, even now, grimy from smoke and soot, unshaven and red-eyed. However, they all grinned, laughed, and talked non-stop. Three of them were younger than me. They were still in college and jumped during the summer to pay for school expenses, making more than enough in a good summer to cover their needs for the term. The college guys were second and third year jumpers while the jumper in charge was a man in his early forties - what seemed to me at the time an impossibly old age.

However, as I learned from our conversation, the challenges were mental as much as physical and this crew was certainly up to the task. As I dropped them off at the district office, a call came for them from dispatch to work yet another fire. They waited at the station while another truck came to pick them up and get them back to their base on the other side of the mountains. What a life.

Storm Warning

One of the oddities about the Pacific Northwest is the weather. I say odd because unlike what most folks may believe, there are actually somewhat predictable periods of incredibly good weather in this part of the country. In the winter, while much of the nation is shivering with terrible cold and buried under snow, most of the Puget Sound region is by comparison quite mild. The snow tends to stay in the mountains and winter temperatures in the lowlands will only occasionally support a snowfall. There also tends to be at least one period in winter when the weather breaks and for a week or two we are treated to gorgeous sunshine and incredible mountain views.

Another surprise for many is the summer weather. In an average year, there are many sunny and warm days in July and August and it is not until late September when we start to see a return to the wet patterns. Rain can still be counted on throughout the summer, as evidenced by the prior stories of misfires on attempted slash burns. It just is not quite as predictable as in winter when one can safely answer the usual question "What's the weather going to be today?" with the single word "Rain," and be right at least ninety percent of the time.

From time to time, even in summer, a low-pressure system will get itself wound up in the Gulf of Alaska, make its way across the North Pacific, and slam hard into the coasts of British Columbia and

Washington. One such storm arrived with gusto on a summer day on the Monte Cristo District.

We were all aware of the coming wet weather since it had been on the news for several days. Meteorologists had been watching this storm as it built far offshore, noting with enthusiasm how it looked more like one of our typical November mid-latitude hurricanes than a storm to be expected in mid-summer. So we had been well warned. The district ranger had even prepared us all for this by putting together a plan for all hands to turn out in response to the major rainfall expected. On the sometimes perilously constructed Forest Service roads, heavy rainfall was of major concern.

When logging roads are built on the side of steep mountains, rainfall has a tendency to wash things away. The roads are well constructed with cut bank side ditches and culverts in order to minimize the effect of runoff. Heavy rain can at times force debris along those ditch lines and plug the culverts. As soon as that happens, water backs up and travels over the road surface. These are dirt and gravel surfaces and in no time at all a road can be heavily damaged by erosional runoff. This was why our Ranger had put together the plan for us to patrol our valuable roads while this storm was pouring water on them. Essentially, we would be on culvert patrol.

The day actually started out nice with clear skies and sun. However, it only took a glance to the western horizon to tell something interesting was going to happen so we all left the ranger station that day with full rain gear, full thermoses and extra food as well as shovels, axes, chainsaws and in some cases even portable radios to supplement our truck's in-dash communications gear. The order of the day was to proceed with whatever business we had previously scheduled and once the rain started to assume patrol of an assigned area, monitoring any water problems and clearing culverts when possible. The chain saws were intended to support our exit plans since in addition to rain, this weather system was going to deliver a bit of wind. Just the idea of something different made for an exciting day. The thing is none of us had counted on this being quite as big a deal as it turned out.

The wind was the real surprise. We got rain for sure and in my rig my partner and I spent quite a few hours digging debris out of plugged culverts while keeping a nervous eye overhead as the trees bent at impossible angles all around us. Sitting in the midst of a clear-cut with no trees either above or below us, we watched as two hundred foot firs were shoved to the ground along the road ahead. We watched in awe as dozens and dozens of old-growth trees were snapped and dropped to the ground. In the road ahead and behind we simply assumed were dozens more that would block us from either moving ahead or retreating back down the mountain toward the main road in the valley. We sat tight, glad to be in the clear as the rain and wind pounded and the timber continued to fall. This went on for a just a short while before the radio came alive.

While my partner and I had been cautiously ensuring we were clear of any possible timber falls, we heard on the radio of one crew that had dispatched early in the day to cruise a timber sale on the side of Green

Mountain, located directly north and above the ranger station. As we sat in our truck, we could look to the west and just make out this mountain through the driving rain. When the storm hit they were deep in the timber with no view to the coming weather. When it arrived, they immediately began a retreat but it took a while to escape to the road. Once on the road, they found their truck crushed under an enormous hemlock tree. Although there was no chance of saving the rig, they did manage to sneak the radio microphone out through one of the shattered windows and call for help before retreating to the relative safety of an open clear-cut a bit farther along the road.

They sat in the driving rain, on the open road and watched as the massive storm continued to drop trees all around them. What I heard on the radio was their initial call for help and then the follow-up calls from the crews that tried to get to them, only to find tree after tree blocking the road. As the storm finally began to subside and it was safe enough to proceed, the rescue crew cut through one tree after another until they reached the mangled green Suburban. The stranded travelers, who had retreated to the clear a bit further up the road, were rescued without further incident and later regaled the rest of us with their harrowing tale over beers.

The story didn't completely end until the forester who was driving that day – Steve – was feted at a going away party when he was transferring to a district in Arizona. As a departing memento from the rest of the district crew, he was awarded a hand-crafted plaque with official Monte Cristo / USFS logos. Attached to it was a small jar containing bits of glass from the shattered windshield of the vehicle they had sacrificed to the mighty summer storm.

A routine summer following that event was wrapped up when I received an award for my work in filling in for the recently transferred post sale forester Captain Pete. Remember, I was struggling to survive on my GS-4 wages of four dollars an hour, so the fact that this award included a check was a huge bonus for me. While I appreciated the fact my efforts were noticed and rewarded, I had to chuckle when the Ranger announced my two hundred and fifty dollar award, particularly when I looked at the accompanying check and saw it had a hundred dollars deducted for taxes. It became the final joke of the season – Willard's one hundred and fifty dollar two hundred and fifty dollar reward.

Winter Again

Forest Service staffing levels are as predictable as the seasons. In the spring, the seasonal hires begin to arrive drifting back like migrating birds. By summer, the district may be twice as populous, or more, as the temporary help fills out work crews for a whole range of projects. Most of this is due to the nature of the work itself. Fire crews, for instance, would have little to do over winter when the entire forest is buried under snow. The same is true for planting and thinning, trail building and campground maintenance. The work force needs to be around only for a specific period of time. The other, less evident advantage to this approach is that it allows the agency to maintain a staffing level of permanent employees that is considerable lower than the actual number of people at work on the district. This is good for political reasons since employment figures tend to focus on full time staff numbers. Depending on how you want to present your budget reports, this can be a handy tool.

I mentioned earlier how the people who make up these seasonal crews have a variety of activities that keep them occupied over the winter. I have worked with a lot of students who use their summers as a way to make money for another term. Their career goals may be to become foresters and return full time, but many of them have completely different goals in mind. Folks that I have known ended up as attorneys, telecommunications technicians, and teachers. Teachers in particular can also be found contributing to the seasonal crews on a number of districts long after their graduation from college. Others have become professional outfitters and guides for fishing and hunting as well as river rafting trips and as ski patrol or ski instructors. Then there is the well-known Wenatchee, Washington photographer whose work you have seen in National Geographic as well as in his own books. Or maybe you are a consumer of the fine Washington wine produced by the man who is now the head winemaker at a well-known winery. We even get to claim a successful politician from the ranks of one-time seasonals at Monte Cristo.

The common thread for this diverse group, though, was that by Thanksgiving, they were all gone. Once again, as the holidays approached, the pace on the District would slow. As more and more people ended their year's work, it grew quieter and quieter. There was a sense of slowly arriving tranquility, knowing that the summer's paperwork would keep the permanent crew busy through the winter months, and for the most part, it would also keep them inside. With the arrival of the winter's first snows, all these people would drift off to their other lives taking with them only memories from the summer in the woods. With the coming of November, the rains began in earnest. The snow, at first seen only on the summits of the surrounding mountains, gradually fell lower and lower. Colors gently changed from the summer's blues and greens to black and white. The valley quietly entered another winter.

Oregon

It was a strangely difficult decision. I had worked as a seasonal employee of the Forest Service for two years when my campaign to secure a permanent position was finally successful and I landed a posting on the Willamette National Forest just to the east of Eugene, Oregon. This was the land of "real" logging and big timber. Not the steep and rocky kind of terrain I was familiar with, but a much gentler country with more of a rolling feel to it. I didn't fully understand why it was not a snap decision to make the transfer until after I made the move.

The Blue River Ranger District was big river country. It straddled the McKenzie River that flowed west toward Eugene. It wasn't an area that included the summit peaks of the Cascades. That honor belonged to the district just to the east of us. Instead, it included thousands and thousands of acres of relatively accessible low to mid-elevation Douglas-fir forest. Most of it was already cut by the time I arrived.

The drainages to both sides of the McKenzie were dammed into stump studded reservoirs - the Blue River Reservoir to the north and the Cougar Reservoir to the south. Between them, the deep waters of the McKenzie River slipped along tree lined meanders as it headed west in search of the Willamette Valley and its even bigger river.

The land rose gently from the riverbank in a series of long, easy slopes that were progressively less timbered the farther away from the tourist highway one traveled. This road carried large numbers of eastbound travelers on their way to Black Butte and Redmond and Bend and Mt. Bachelor. The cars were filled with tourists that wanted to believe their National Forests were still full of trees. To enhance this belief, much of the old growth was left standing in areas that were within sight of the highway. But, as soon as the pavement disappeared from view, the trees were gone.

When I was working on this district, the Willamette supplied more timber than any other national forest in the country. Period. What pockets of old growth there were that were left were remote and isolated, and relatively small in size. At least these small stands were as isolated as is possible in this part of the Cascades. Perhaps it is because I was first introduced to the Cascade Range in the more rugged and less developed northern reaches, but I was shocked at the sights that awaited me when I first arrived.

If for no other reason than they are closer to the existing population centers of California, it is understandable that the Oregon forests would be more heavily used and be more impacted than the terrain farther north. Add to that the much less rugged topography and the resultant lower expense of extracting the resource and the reason it was more heavily logged becomes clear. The climate is also milder as one travels farther south with longer growing seasons. The result of all of this is the Oregon logging experience.

I started my time on the Blue River District doing work that was familiar to me – tree planting inspection and reforestation stocking surveys. Given the huge number of acres that had been cut on this forest, there was plenty of work to do. In fact, there was so much of this to do I soon found myself limited to just these two jobs.

It was February when I started and the contract tree planting work was just getting underway since winter left this area a bit earlier than I was accustomed to. Most days I was out the door of my nice little McKenzie River-front cabin by 5a.m. I made the short drive to the ranger station and unlocked the tree cooler where I would load up several thousand seedlings in their craft paper bags and then drive to the day's location where I would meet up with the planting crew. These were some hard working folks. They started the day at first light and usually worked until it was near dark. Many of them counted on tree planting for a big part of their yearly income so they wanted to make maximum progress when they could. I was needed on the job site the entire time they worked, so my days would typically run twelve hours or more. This went on for seven days a week for a couple of months until warmer weather caused things to slow down a bit.

My workweek then returned to a normal five-day routine but my work was now exclusively stocking surveys with my days all spent in recently logged clear-cuts. I missed the old growth and the big timber I had gotten used to exploring in my last position. In spite of that, it was still fun to be in a new area learning additional details about the business of forestry and the oddities of the Forest Service.

Tree Climbing

As spring turned to summer I was offered a chance to go a bit farther south on the Willamette National Forest to the Dorena Tree Improvement Center just outside of Cottage Gove, Oregon. There were some interesting things going on at Dorena, including studies for determining disease resistance in trees, research into several serious diseases affecting forest health and a seed storage facility. For me, the reason I came was to attend the Dorena Tree Climbing Program.

Tree climbing in the Forest Service is done for several reasons. The first and most common reason is to harvest cones out of the trees in order to collect the seeds to provide stock for the many replanting efforts taking place around the forest. This was an area I was recently very familiar with and I understood the need to select appropriate trees to ensure healthy stock from specific regional and altitudinal locations. There are additional research and wildlife needs within many government agencies that require the ability to scale safely the massive old growth found along the Pacific Coast and in the Cascades and elsewhere. This program, which I was to attend, was held at a facility literally just down the road from my current posting. I jumped at the opportunity to spend my time doing something different from the ongoing stocking surveys.

I had been introduced to rock climbing some years before from a friend who was from Kalispell, Montana. He had dragged me up several Cascade peaks and shown me the basics needed to avoid most bad outcomes, so I felt I had a bit of an advantage for the Dorena program. After all, climbing is climbing and I knew how to tie a few knots and what to do when belaying a climbing partner. From those days of scaling cliffs in the mountains, I had experienced much greater exposure than I was ever going to see in any Douglas-fir so I entered the program with great enthusiasm and some confidence in my ability to handle the heights. Along with a dozen or so other folks from both the Forest Service and National Park Service as well as a couple of Oregon state agencies, I spent a full week learning to manage the specialized gear needed to climb these big beautiful trees. I did well enough that on my return to the Blue River District, my supervisor informed me I had been requested to return as an instructor. After a couple more weeks of grinding out stocking surveys, I was able to make another journey south to Dorena.

I spent two weeks training climbers. I never let any of them know I had only been through the course myself just a couple of weeks before, operating on the principle that they needed me to instill confidence in them that I knew what I was doing. It was also true that even though it was not much, I did at least know a bit more than they did. At least until the last day when we all became equally experienced.

I first taught them to climb using the traditional spurs and flip line. This is the method most commonly seen and utilizes spikes, or spurs, strapped to your legs and a rope, which is wrapped around the trunk of the tree and then "flipped" upward, or down as the climber moves up or down the trunk. This is a quick way to the top but obviously, it will cause damage to the tree from the spurs. If you are only climbing a tree one time, or at least infrequently, this is an acceptable way to go. It is also largely harmless on the bigger fir trees since they have such thick bark.

There is a forestry management technique that involves identifying genetically superior trees based on growth characteristics. These trees are selected by a combination of visual inspection and physical measurements and are marked with paint and located on a map for easy return in the future. These trees serve as an annual cone and seed collection location to provide the best nursery stock for replanting. Picking these outstanding specimens ensures the best seedlings will be produced. Since these trees are going to be climbed every year, using spurs may not be the best option since the holes left behind in the bark may allow the introduction of insects and disease. For this situation, when there is concern over ongoing damage to a tree, we provided training on some alternate methods for getting to the top branches and those choice cones that always seem to be up high.

In all events, the use of spurs or any other method is only intended to get the climber to the branches where they continue hand over hand in much the same way we climbed trees as children. The difference is that at one hundred plus feet off the ground, certain precautions will be needed to ensure a safe climb and a safe return to the ground.

For some trees, ladders will serve to get you to the branches as well as spurs. These ladders, however, are not your standard hardware store variety extension ladders, but rather specially constructed sectional ladders that attach together end to end, allowing the climber to "build" a ladder from the ground up, attaching it to the tree with a chain or rope device. Because they are attached directly to the trunk of the tree and held in place by chains or ropes wrapped around the trunk, the ladder is vertical. This is unlike standing an extension ladder up along your house in order to get to the gutters to clean leaves out. These Swiss-made ladders can be quite intimidating when you are some distance up and standing on a narrow ladder attached close to the trunk. The same flip line that is used for climbing with spurs is used here to ensure you are attached to the trunk.

Climbing footplates and various friction devices also were trained to allow a climber alternate, frequent access upward. These are clumsy and often expensive devices but we still taught our climbers to use them. I have never actually seen them in use on the big trees in the Northwest, but presumably, somewhere there are Forest Service employees using them.

A considerable amount of time was spent when the student was in the branches to ensure the climber was fully trained on ropes and knots and safety procedures. I spent most of the latter half of each week sitting on a high branch of our instruction tree, advising climbers as they made their way up by the various means mentioned and then demonstrating techniques to them once they were in the branches. And then, finally, the real fun took place when we taught them how to rappel back to the ground.

The student was fitted with a harness of the type used by Forest Service Helitack crews. These crews exit a hovering helicopter and descend via rope in order to reach the ground in the area of a fire that allows no other access. We equipped the trainees with the same rappelling device used by these helicopter fire crews and then made sure they were comfortable in using the gear on the journey down. We taught them to use the Sky Genie descender and how to wrap the specially made rope around the central cylinder of this device in order to control friction on the rope. The more wraps of rope, the greater the friction as the rope slid around the cylinder and the slower the descent. Fewer wraps and you'd better be prepared for a quick trip down. We taught them to respect the rope on which their safety depended. Stepping on a climbing rope is a cardinal sin. At the end of the session, we either certified them or sent them home with some things to think about.

Of particular interest to me is the profile of the typical successful climber. Or I should say the complete lack of a profile of a typical successful climber. There are people who are simply terrified of heights and exposure. And there are people that are not. I have seen several very rugged outdoor types, very macho guys who turned to jelly at ten feet in the air. I learned there is no value judgment to be made. They should not climb and I would tell them that. The only way to find out who was capable and who was not was to put them on a rope and watch what happened. I had a wonderful experience at Dorena.

Alone On the Hill

Summer came early that year in Oregon. As a result, things dried out by June and preparations were underway for slash burning. With the amount of timber cutting taking place on this district, there was a lot of slash to clean up so the fire crew here was much bigger than the one I had worked with on the Monte Cristo District. The folks on this crew were much more likely to spend time fighting fires than my first station's group given the more moderate rainfall in the central Cascades of Oregon and the generally drier summers. The key skill on the Monte Cristo, as I mentioned earlier, was frequently the ability to get fires started given the wet conditions. No such problem existed on the Blue River District.

In this environment, there was every chance for things to get out of hand quickly so precautions were particularly important and procedures were much more closely followed here. I had taken time in the spring to attend fire school classes and take the required tests for my "red card", the authorization for wild land firefighting. With this official sanction, I was assigned to help with the slash burning activity as it got underway in early summer. I considered this a delight as it meant a break from the endless reforestation stocking surveys.

Having had some experience at lighting with a drip torch – I may have left out the details of my near miss on the Double Eagle fire when they quizzed me regarding my background – I was put on a crew and worked a couple of small, early season slash fires with nothing of particular interest happening. Things went well on both fires and they were soon forgotten. Fire number three was a different matter.

This logging unit was good sized, close to one hundred acres, and on a very steep east facing hill. Along the southern boundary, running the entire distance bottom to top was a young stand of replanted fir, what we called "reprod", that was about ten or fifteen years old. This was one of those very dense, Christmas tree sized collections of regrowth that had not yet been pre-commercially thinned. It contained a lot of potential fuel since it was packed with the young green trees. These can burn like crazy once they get started, the fire forcing water out of the needles and resin out of the trunks and cones and drying them ahead of ignition so they practically explode. We were all very aware of the potential along this boundary and had inch and a half hose lain top to bottom with portable pumps positioned in the creek that ran along the base of the clear-cut we intended to burn. We posted a number of people along the fire line on the south side edge with instructions to be alert for any spotting and to extinguish any fire immediately. They were also advised to call for help quickly if needed.

Along the north side was old growth, a beautiful stand of fir with some hemlock and a fabulous stand of red cedar along the bottom where it was cooler and wetter from shade and the creek. These were big trees, hundreds of years old with very little understory because of the lack of sunlight reaching the forest floor there. We were less concerned about this line given the lack of fuels on the ground. We assigned only a couple of spotters to work this line.

After some tragic wildfires in the past years, most fire crews today equip everyone on site with a radio. I suspect the same may be true of slash crews given the inexpensive radios to be had now. On this Oregon fire, however, radios were at a premium. They were bulky in those days, about the size of quart of milk and quite expensive. As a result, not everyone carried them. With our concern over the southern line along the reprod, we made sure everyone there had a radio in case of trouble so all the crew along that side could call for help. We scattered the remainder amongst the rest of the crew. Our drip torch crew had one, there seemed to be no need for more.

We started slowly, gauging the fire behavior before letting things get too far out of hand, and soon felt confident in our ability to avoid any problems with the south side reprod. As we picked up speed and the fire heated up a bit, we were getting good intensity but keeping things under control. At about two thirds of the way down the hill, we were chased down by one of the crew that was working the line along the old growth who, with some urgency, told us the fire had moved into the timber there and was starting to heat up. I handed off my drip torch to the crew member in front of me and went with the spotter back to the fire line along the old growth. Things were indeed burning – even more ambitiously than he had managed to let on. I also noted that the fuel load at the bottom of the hill, in the cedar, was considerably more than what we had scouted out near the top when making the original assignments. The fire was in the cedar.

Neither of us had a radio. Noting the nervousness of the rookie that had called me over, I took his tool, a Pulaski, which is a combination ax and grub hoe, and sent him to reconnect with my drip torch crew and have them radio for more help to work this side. He took off and I headed into the timber and started scratching line around the nearest spot fire, digging frantically along the uphill of the small blaze while trying at the same time to kick dirt on the flames.

I seemed to have contained the first spot fire in a small circle about twenty feet in diameter when I moved to the next, a bit farther into the timber and burning next to a large cedar. The trunk was starting to catch fire on that tree so I hurried over and dealt with that one. Looking uphill, I saw another fire just above me that needed my attention. Then I looked downhill and there was another blaze. Fortunately, it appeared as if all these spots were still quite small and I was able to contain them as I came to them, although I was aware there were more fires burning than I was able to manage effectively. I simply took on whatever was immediately next to me, circling it with line and kicking dirt when I could.

This exhausting work continued for a good forty-five minutes before I realized my spotter had not returned from his trip to the drip torch crew. No one else had shown up either. I looked around and noted there was no one else in sight. I was completely alone. Upon realizing this, I stopped digging and started looking around a bit more intently.

There was fire everywhere. I was a good two hundred feet into the timber from the fire line and things were burning on all sides of me. In some places, it was starting to burn with some degree of enthusiasm. I could also see that the clear-cut on the other side of the line was burning energetically so I assumed my drip torch crew had completed lighting and must have moved on. I also noted that with the heavy volume of smoke my limit of visibility was just a few feet beyond the edge of the timber into the now actively burning clear-cut. There was no one in sight anywhere.

Every direction I looked was now on fire. Suddenly, I found myself very afraid. While there was no wall of flame, I was completely surrounded and there was no obvious good way out. It did occur to me that my best choice would be to clear out quickly before I actually became trapped since presumably no one knew exactly where I was. I made for deeper timber, thinking I would be out of the active burn area more quickly that way and in short order I was able to look both uphill and down and see only trees. The fire was all behind me now. I did not know what was ahead so continuing that way did not seem a good idea. I knew it was a very long way uphill to the road, and I remembered that the road end was in the clear-cut. The road did not extend into this stand of old growth, so going uphill I would not necessarily be able to tell when I was at road level. I did not like that option. I also figured uphill would be a bad option since fire travels fast uphill - much faster than I could.

I headed downhill for the creek. There was still active fire on my right. I could not see through the fire and timber to the clear-cut but I knew it wasn't far. I also knew that once I was below the clear-cut I could reconnect to a fire line on one side of the clear-cut or the other. I reached the creek in just a few minutes and started making my way along it until I was below the clear-cut, where I saw fire as far down as the creek. My torch crew was nowhere in sight so I assumed they were on the far side, along the reprod. I headed there.

On reaching the far fire line, I finally found other people, one of whom had a radio. Using it, I called in the report of what was happening in the old growth and was surprised to find out no one knew about it. My spotter had apparently not stressed the urgency enough so there were no reinforcements on the way.

That changed quickly when word reached the FMO. A large group was assembled and immediately dispatched to move down the line on the old growth side where they worked until well into the night to contain and extinguish the many fires burning there. It was far enough along that a number of snags had to be dropped back into the clear-cut to avoid having the fire spread even farther. In the end, it all came out well.

I, for one, was glad to be done with that fire. The feeling of being alone in that stand of big trees, turning in a circle and seeing fire in all directions, stayed with me for a long time.

Independence

I had been concerned for some time about my inability to get into one of the specific fields I had targeted when studying during my university days. My intention all along had been to pursue some aspect of wildlife biology and joining the Forest Service had simply been a means to get my foot in the door. I always assumed one needed to become part of the organization first and then find a way to carve out the desired niche.

Even though I had already overcome numerous obstacles in learning how to navigate the maze of Civil Service hiring, I was beginning to question my ability to shift from the forestry technician track I seemed to have been assigned. The longer I stayed in this position, the more likely I was to be viewed simply as a technician. All I could imagine was seeing my chances of landing a position as a biologist diminishing with the passage of time. Most of the work I was doing on the Blue River district was reforestation stocking surveys associated with the post-sale activity I had learned from my prior work. Given the amount of logging, there would continue to be large acreage to be replanted every year so it was easy to see how the need for experienced personnel to manage the planting and reforestation efforts would continue to exist. I began to think it time to consider other options.

From my first season and introduction to contract administration following the early departure of my supervisor, I had become acquainted with a number of independent contractors who did tree planting and pre-commercial thinning as well as other activities. I was keenly aware of the earnings potential in those positions having signed off on a few contracts during that time. It was substantially more than I was making in my current job, which barely provided me with enough money for survival.

I contacted an outfit from Seattle to check into possibilities. Bear Paw Forestry had done some work for me on the Monte Cristo District and after a couple of conversations, I decided to sign on with them and give it a shot.

Given the difficulty in securing a permanent posting with the Forest Service, my co-workers at the Blue River District were stunned when I resigned. Their disbelief did not help my worry that I might be making the wrong decision, but keeping an image of piles of dollars firmly in mind, I packed my truck with the few belongings I had and headed north to Seattle. I was starting over.

My initial work for Bear Paw was doing what I loved best – timber stand exams. They had a major contract to survey a large number of timber stands and needed the experience I could bring to the group. For the balance of that summer, I explored areas of the Cascades I had not seen before, along the eastern slopes of the mountains. I worked on various districts of the Wenatchee National Forest and explored out of the way places in the Snoqualmie Pass area and spent a couple of months north of there in the Lake Wenatchee area. This region was very appealing to me and is now the location of my mountain cabin – Black Bear Lodge – which is a just short distance from the lake.

Having spent all my time up to then working on west side forests, I was fascinated by the differences I encountered in dealing with the stands located on the drier east side of the range. Since most moisture from the incoming Pacific storms gets squeezed out as the air is forced up over the mountains, the quantity of precipitation drops dramatically once you clear the crest of the mountains. In these stands, I first encountered the ponderosa pine forest.

For doing this work, one begins with a collection of maps and aerial photos. The area to be surveyed is marked on both map and photo by the Forest Service delineating the boundaries. Details of the contract specify requirements for how thoroughly one must look things over. I would establish and draw grid lines on the photos based on the number of desired survey points. The crossing of these lines established the location of each plot to be measured. Once that was done, I could physically identify the specific plot locations as they were placed on the photo. The trick was to find those exact locations on the ground.

Based on the scale of the map and photos, I could determine the exact distance between points, including finding the starting point from some identifiable location on the road or trail. On a flat surface, one can easily determine how many paces are required to travel a specified distance. To do so you simply use a measuring tape and mark off, say 100 feet. You then walk using your normal pace and count the number of steps it takes to cover this distance. This method allowed me to locate plot centers by pacing to measure distance. A small problem arises, of course, when you are no longer on flat ground, or when you have to climb over fallen logs, or cross streams. And then there are the frequent cliffs. By using a combination of actual physical measurements, (I always carried a one hundred foot tape) and by measuring the slope angle and applying some of that geometry I learned in school, I was able to arrive at my desired location with a high degree of accuracy. This accuracy was important in order to maintain the randomness needed to provide a true view of the timber and terrain. It would be easy to stroll along until finding a nice flat, open area and establish the plot there. Unfortunately, if that flat open area were the only one in a five acre area, the results of my measurements would be essentially useless for the planning purposes for which the stand exam was being conducted. Today I imagine how much simpler all this would be with the advent of GPS.

Upon establishing the point, or plot, I would measure all the trees in a specified circle and by using optical instruments that would measure a tree diameter I was able to determine which trees within sight were "in" or "out" of the plot. The winners, those that landed within the plot, were measured for height and drilled for age and observations were made as to general vigor. Additional collection of data included comments on other plant life, slope, any hazards or notable physical features and comments as to what was visible in the plot. All this information, when collated and viewed as a whole, gave the foresters enough information to make management decisions regarding the area.

I loved doing this work whether in sun or rain with or without bugs. I almost always felt as though I was the first human to walk the ground, which I'm sure was usually untrue. It is just that there were so many places I went that I could find no logical reason for anyone else to have visited. My conclusion was that I surely must have been the true pioneer. In some cases, this was probably true. There were many memorable days that summer working with Bear Paw. There were sights, sounds, and even smells that remain with me to this day, but one day in particular stands out.

Late in the season, we were working on some timber tracts that were located in an area north of the Wenatchee River and east of Leavenworth. It is an area where the forest begins dramatically thinning out due to lack of rainfall and the timber gets smaller and sparser on south slopes. The north slopes in the area are a mix of small grand fir and Douglas-fir, none of which gets very big but finds life a bit easier in the zone out of the hot summer sun. The south slopes consist almost entirely of Ponderosa Pine, sparsely growing on the hot, dry sunny side.

The entire area I am referring to burned to the ground in 2004 in a series of near-disastrous lightning-caused fires. When I was there, it was still a living forest and I recall crawling through the area and commenting on the incredible fuel loads on the ground. It seemed as though a hundred years of deadfall was piled up and at times I'd walk for a hundred yards from log to log, my boots never touching the ground. However, at the time, it was still a fairly healthy stand. Today, it is gone.

We had arrived at this location via a beat up and mostly abandoned logging road and were able to drive quite far on what must have been double-lane tracks left by hunters that had been kept somewhat open by years of travel on the way to deer hunts. I managed to get my small pickup to a nice spot on top of a hill that had an unobstructed view in all directions. That was where we made camp. We worked out of there for several days.

It was August and hot and the skies were clear. On about the third day there was just a hint of building clouds on the far western horizon so I put up a tent rainfly over the back of my open pickup bed where I had tossed my sleeping bag. That would provide me with protection in case anything wet developed, but I was annoyed that I lost my view of the stars. In any case, thinking it to be better safe than sorry, I opted for the cover in case it rained.

Sometime deep into the night I was awakened by a light. Tired from a day of crawling up and down hills and over the mountains of downed timber, it took me a bit to wake up. I sat up in the bed of the truck and could see that someone was shining a light across the top of my rainfly. The light was so bright it had disturbed my sleep. I slipped on an unlaced pair of boots and climbed out of the truck bed to confront the interloper and his dazzling flashlight. But what I saw was not some midnight adventurer at all. The sky was ablaze.

I had never seen anything like it. From directly overhead all the way to the horizon on the north, the sky was quivering with brilliant white sheets of light. It was as though I was looking at sheer, white curtains hanging from the sky and was watching them wave in the wind. Each movement caused the white sheets to flare up brighter or to dim a bit giving me the sense of looking at liquid light. It was as if I were under the ocean, watching waves above me with white sunlight bouncing and slicing and turning. It was the single most incredible view of the Aurora Borealis I have ever seen. And it was as white as a spotlight.

I stayed up the rest of the night, until the liquid sky faded with the arrival of the sun. It never did rain.

Early the next year I worked with Bear Paw on tree planting contracts, bringing my two years of industrial planting experience from Scott Paper and urging the crew to new levels in terms of production. Since we were essentially paid by the tree, the more enthusiasm mustered the more money we all made. All the while this was going on I was working to establish my own company and with the blessing of my employer I began bidding on contracts for my new outfit, Island Forestry. The name was chosen because at the time I was living on an island in the north of Puget Sound. My first "hit" was to be a memorable one, but it was not, as I had hoped, doing stand exams.

The First Thinning Contract

After about three years of working for the Forest Service, it occurred to me that something was drastically wrong. I had been spending many of my days as a contract administrator. I like to use that term because it sounds so much more inclusive than what it was I actually did which simply contract compliance inspection. In this capacity, my job was to follow contract laborers around as they did their work and insure they complied, more or less, with the terms of the contract they were performing. What this really meant was that I had to make certain they planted the trees root side down and they cut the reprod when precommercial thinning with some semblance of order. It was important that they actually cut the tree down at ground level and did not just lop off the top so it looked good from a distance.

For this effort, I received my GS-4 wage of four dollars an hour. And here is where I knew something was wrong. I had a college education, considered myself a reasonably bright individual, a quick learner, and had waded my way through the very competitive hiring process to achieve the permanent position I recently held. While doing these contract inspections I was surrounded by people who in many cases had little or no education and many with no discernible skills beyond the running of a chain saw. I also noted in these groups a few people not unlike myself. The interesting part is that in all cases, these people were making two or three times as much money for their time as I was and sometimes considerably more. I had begun to wonder if possibly my measure of intelligence was flawed. Using these facts and my somewhat questionable logic, I had hired on the prior year with one of these contractors and was now determined to go into business for myself and leave this low-paying Forest Service game behind.

It was about ten months after leaving the Forest Service that I actually accomplished this feat with the formation of Island Forestry and the acquisition of my first government contract. The company was so named because at the time I lived on an island in Puget Sound. I decided that the first line of business to go into was whichever type of contract I could land initially. This well thought out approach turned me into a pre-commercial thinner. Two hundred and seventy-one acres of young trees awaited me on the very district that I had worked on initially - the Monte Cristo. Since I had submitted many bids for a number of projects on several different districts on more than one National Forest, it is more than ironic that I should have received this one first and reconnected with my original work area and many of my old co-workers.

In reality, this was more than a bit fortunate for me. First of all, I knew the district very well so all of the areas I was to work were familiar to me. I knew all of the roads and all of the camping areas so it was an easy transition from government employee to government contractor. Secondly, and much more significantly, I knew all of the people that would administer and inspect the contract. I had just worked with them for three seasons. In any case that called for judgment, this had to work in my favor. That definitely seemed to me to be a big plus.

There was one small hitch to all of this, however. Although I had for several years followed a number of different thinning crews around and done inspections and performed the various contract administration activities, I had never actually cut a single tree as a pre-commercial thinner, let alone two hundred and seventy one acres. As a result, all of my numbers were based upon my best guess, which was generated from my experience of watching other people, most of whom, unfortunately for me, were experienced thinners.

When things did not turn out quite as lucratively as I had hoped, I had to admit that this might have been as a result of my total lack of hands-on experience. That they turned out at all, I can only attribute to a combination of luck, complete grit and determination, and countless days of daylight to dark drudgery that made me all but weep for the good ol' days of being a Forest Service "drone".

In spite of the difficulties encountered along the way, this did at last represent the official beginning of my independent business. It got underway finally in late April when the snow backed off enough for me to begin work with my shiny new Stihl chain saws and my two shiny new employees, both of whom had approximately less experience than me. If that handicap weren't enough, the first day, in fact the first week, no, let's face it, the first month was spent in driving rain.

We had probably completed two hours on the first day when we sustained our first injury. Mark, who we started calling Mangled Mark shortly after we got underway, was prone to injury as I was to learn.

The minor cut that he sustained on his thigh the first day led me on another trip to the loggers supply store where I bought three pairs of Kevlar reinforced chaps that were designed to drag the speeding chain to a stop just before it managed to reach the meaty part of your quadriceps. The mental security provided by these items worked wonders for our progress from then on. While they protected the most vulnerable part of the body while running the saws, "Mangled" still managed to find ways to nick and cut himself with amazing regularity.

The most memorable part of this work is that it is horrible from start to finish. So horrible in fact that even when you are done you're not done. There are a number of things you take home with you. Home in this case being the inside of a wet tent, or later, when we were more desperate, the inside of the rented motor home which we fondly referred to as "the MH". The first thing that accompanies you home every night is the aroma. It's a combination of sweat, rain, saw exhaust and pine pitch. The saw exhaust shrouds you all day long and manages to seep into every rain-soaked pore. After an all-day bout with this environment, one tends to forget that this work is in the fresh mountain air. The smell of a thinner rivals the smell of swamp mud that is disturbed by a footprint with the disgusting, foul smell released for the first time in maybe a million years. A thinner smells like the old air inside a tire.

The second thing taken home is a series of painful body parts, the most obvious being the result of holding a chain saw all day. This causes hand cramps of monumental proportions. Even after months of doing this work and having achieved whatever degree of fitness I would achieve from the work, I would awaken in the mornings with my fists clenched and all but immovable from fatigue. It would take several minutes of flexing and stretching to be able to use them normally. It mattered little because as soon as I fired the machine up once more I would spend the next twelve or fourteen hours with my hands gripping the saw and setting the stage for a repeat performance the next morning.

Thinning is mindless, brutal, intensely difficult physical labor. It is the most difficult work I have ever done. There must be something that is worse, perhaps breaking rocks in the August sun on an Alabama chain gang, but I have no experience in that matter. I can only say that at least it would be drier on the chain gang. Working while you are shrouded in your rain gear, the outside air temperature about thirty-three degrees, trying to remain upright on the side of hill so steep that you can barely hang on, can only be described as not much fun.

It was not just Mark that got hurt. Others had their share of injuries in this game too. One of the crew sliced his leg nearly off at the ankle one afternoon when he became more than normally distracted by the difficulties of his divorce and let his attention wander at just the wrong moment. The inside of his leg just above the ankle was so deeply sliced that he was unable to walk. Fortunately for him, Big John was big enough to toss him over a shoulder and muscle his way down the steep hill to the road complete with a dose of encouraging comments.

"Hell, this ain't nothin' compared to some of the places I packed guys out of in 'Nam. And nobody's shootin' at us here."

Most of the injuries were minor and at times almost humorous. How do you fall down into a huckleberry bush and pierce your eyelid clear through with a branch without touching the eyeball? Falling off a log and splitting the one gallon plastic gas bottle, soaking his clothing, Ozzie didn't let that stop him. He shucked his trousers and climbed into just his rain gear. He finished the day with his pants hanging on the outside of his pack to air out.

Our friend with the sliced ankle was also the one who, having healed up enough to stand, dropped a residual old growth hemlock on top of Mangled Mark and me as we stood, unsuspecting, on the edge of the area we had just cut through. He dropped it on top of us while following along in our staggered line and couldn't see us from his location. Mark didn't see the tree coming at all. I got just enough of a glimpse that I had made a move to back away when it hit me, knocking me nearly senseless and into a heap on the ground below the gravel berm that Mark and I were standing on. Hardhat on the ground beside me, the big saw still running on the other side of the berm, I looked up to see Mark holding his leg and grimacing. The tree had knocked him backward and then crushed his lower leg as it landed on his bent knee. This time Big John was silent as we carried the groaning man, bone sticking out of his splinted leg, out to the road. The codeine I had from a recent dentist visit held him until we made the two hour drive out to help. This was the low point for this summer. It wasn't the end, though. There was still Gene-Gene-The-Thinnin'-Machine.

Having sustained a number of losses, with many players out with serious injuries as well as a collection of sprains and bruises and cuts and whacks and contusions, the completion of the contract was in jeopardy. I was seriously short-handed and seriously short on time. Not that I didn't care about these poor guys that had been working for me - of course I did. If I didn't finish this contract I might become one of them soon enough. Mostly, though, I was concerned about the financial liability I would incur by defaulting on the contract. Not only would I not make all of the money I had dreamed myself into, I would also be responsible for the differential between my bid and what it cost the government to get the work done by another crew. The real difference between a small business doing contracting for the Forest Service and a defense contractor doing business with the government is that the defense contractor has lawyers to explain away the cost overruns and delays. The small businessperson has only himself to blame for trying to compete in a low-cost provider environment. In addition, the small businessperson does not have the attorneys.

In an effort to avoid this disaster, I began working fourteen or more hour days seven days a week. That would have been enough by itself to wear me down, but the area I was working at the time was inaccessible by truck due to logging activity so I was also hiking in a mile every day, carrying gas and saws and equipment. My only remaining working partner at this time was Dan, who like me, was not bright enough to know to abandon a sinking ship and somehow stuck it out. One evening, just as it was getting dark at the end of another grinding day, we encountered two men walking in on the road as we were walking out.

"You Dennis Willard?" the taller one asked me. I was surprised to see anyone at all let alone someone who knew my name. He introduced himself as Gene Green and described himself as a thinner. And he was looking for work. My heart, which up to that point has been somewhere around the tops of my boots, rose to a more pleasant elevation. We talked for a bit and it turned out that while he was the much needed relief that I sought, he came with some baggage. Mainly that he didn't have any equipment or any money to buy it. Out of desperation, I arranged to provide him and his crew with new saws and gas and put them to work a few days later in the adjoining unit of twenty-some acres, which was the final area of work on the contract. He was to repay me for the saws out of his final pay for which I would withhold the funds and he would keep the saws. If everything went according to plan, I might actually complete the contract and perhaps even finish it on time.

In short order, Gene-Gene-the-Thinnin'-Machine and his accomplices were happily working away. After I completed a couple of quick inspections it became apparent that he knew what he was doing, in fact much more so than I did. Unbelievably we actually completed the project ahead of the final date. It seemed that in no time at all, I had finished the last of the unit I was working, Gene and his crew finished theirs, the Forest Service inspectors proclaimed it a job well done and the final papers were signed. I paid Gene for his part less the cost of the saws, we shook hands and said goodbye. As you may have suspected already, that was not the end of the story.

Having survived some five months of precommercial thinning, untold gallons of gas and quarts of oil, countless hours of sharpening chain, repairing various broken parts both on saws and people, I was in a state of near bliss as I started my next contract. This time it was to be timber stand exams which used no power tools, so no noise, just old-growth timber and a few small measuring implements for determining height and diameter and age of the gloriously beautiful trees on the east side of the Cascades. Shortly after starting this project I had driven to the nearest inhabited area to call home and check on the status of the family and to see if any money had arrived from my earlier ventures. My wife immediately told me,

"I'm sure glad you called. The criminal investigator for the Mt. Baker National Forest has been calling here; he wants to talk to you as soon as he can. He wouldn't say about what but he did say it was very important." I froze. What had I done? Was I in violation of some aspect of the thinning contract? Had I inadvertently left one of my crew in the woods? What? With my fears magnifying, I dialed the number that he left me and asked for the man who had called me.

"Do you know a Gene Green?" he asked me when I introduced myself. As he began explaining to me why he wanted to talk, I didn't know quite what to say. At first, all I could think of was that at least it wasn't me he was after. It seems that shortly after I handed Gene the check for the work he had done for me, he disappeared from sight. At least from the sight of the two guys who had been working with him on the project. They got neither the saws nor the cash they had been promised. Not satisfied with that take, on his way out of the valley he made a stop at the ranger station, which was closed at the late hour of his departure, and relieved the warehouse of several more saws, various hand tools and an undetermined amount of fuel for his truck. He did manage to find a bank and cash the check from me before he left the area the next morning. That might well have been the end of Gene Green for all concerned had he not made that fateful stop at the 7-11 in Eugene, Oregon where he found himself less adept at robbery than he had been at thinning. In the Lane County lockup, it was discovered that Gene Green was actually named Bob Johnson. The alias belonged to his step-father.

Tree Planting Again

Shortly after the start of the new year I decided to add tree planting to the list of contract jobs I did. Given my extensive experience in this area, I was certain I could bid these jobs accurately and hopefully do pretty well as a business. Unlike my thinning "experience", I actually knew this work. I went to my old employer, Scott Paper Company, and inquired about the possibility of doing some planting for them and was rewarded with a contract for more work than I ever imagined. The biggest problem I then faced was in securing a crew.

Before signing the contract and completing all the necessary plans, I felt it prudent to begin searching for suitable planters to join me. I paid a visit to the local state Employment Security office and explained my needs to them. What followed was an adventure of sorts. I was summoned back to their office in about a week to interview their first round of selected candidates. Because I didn't specifically ask them, I'm uncertain what criteria the Employment Security folks used to choose their applicants, but I strongly suspect the only job requirement was "are you unemployed?" Not a single person I met with in that office had any experience at tree planting. For that matter, most of them had never even worked outdoors. I found it difficult to imagine that in a forestry related economy such as existed in Washington at the time I could not find any experienced hands, so I politely thanked the government office and went on my way.

After tracking down everyone I knew that I had worked with in the past, I collected a dozen or so numbers and started phoning around. Between those direct contacts, and people those contacts knew, I soon had a crew of twenty reasonably experienced planters lined up and ready to go as soon as the weather cooperated.

In the same way I had to equip my thinning crew with saws and accessories, I needed to secure planting tools for this group. I ordered a collection of hoedads and planter's bags from an outfit in Mississippi that was the largest company around at the time. Once outfitted, I waited eagerly for the season to get underway.

When the snows finally melted out enough in the lower elevations, we were able to collect the crew and get underway. In short order it became clear to me that this was going to be a much more lucrative proposition than thinning. On a per-day basis, I was able to make five or ten or sometimes twenty times as much money as on thinning, The season would be shorter for planting than thinning, but after that first contract I was a confirmed tree planning contractor. We completed about six hundred acres for Scott Paper that first year. A few of the crew, which for the most part proved to be an outstanding group, stayed with me for the summer thinning work.

Timber Stand Exams

At the same time I was chasing down tree planting work I began investigating doing contract timber stand exams as well. I submitted a few unsuccessful bids and began to get a feel for the market when I finally landed my first contract. It was located on the Wenatchee National Forest for the Cle Elum Ranger District.

As it had been with tree planting, I had significant experience at doing this work so I was confident in both the bid I had submitted as well as in the likelihood I was going to enjoy this work. The truth is I had no idea just how much fun it would be until it was actually underway.

I brought along one helper on this job to prevent being alone in the more remote areas. He had a good background in forestry but had to be trained to do this work. He was a capable student and soon we were making excellent progress on our commitments.

As I described elsewhere, this was very enjoyable work because to a large degree it consisted of hiking through the woods and climbing the mountains. While it is true we almost never were able to use trails since we needed to follow a strict pre-determined line to establish our plots, it was nonetheless very enjoyable to travel through the woods, always wondering if we were the first people to visit a particular place. I realize that's probably a bit silly, but in truth we were often in locations I simply could not imagine anyone ever setting foot on before. Maybe hunters, maybe at one time prospectors, but many of these locations just seemed so incredibly out of the way, I still have to wonder if we weren't the first.

The reward for pressing through the brush, and climbing uphill against thickets of vine-maple and devils club, were views that were spectacular and quiet and solitude of unimaginable character. The evenings were often spent around a campfire, cooking dinner and drinking beer, watching the light fade and trying to imagine where one could possibly be that was more enjoyable than the exact spot we occupied at that moment. Somehow, over the passing of time, the bugs and the heat and the fatigue just fade from my memory.

I have memories of sitting along the shores of Lake Cle Elum in camp, of hiking along Cooper Lake, of discovering a steel barrel a mile deep in the woods with no idea of how it got there (fell from a helicopter?) of hiking up a closed and abandoned road along Fortune Creek to views of the Stuart Range, all still fresh in my mind.

Superior Tree Selection

As a climbing instructor in Oregon, I would discuss with my students the techniques needed to scale a two hundred foot tall tree in order to retrieve the cones. These cones were gently lowered to the ground in burlap sacks and taken to one of the regional Forest Service nurseries. In the Northwest, that is the Wind River Nursery located along the Columbia River just upstream from Portland. Here the cones were processed and the seeds removed and planted. Millions of tree seedlings are produced there as a result.

For each collection of cones, the resultant trees were noted as to species, location of collection, and elevation of the source tree. Once the seeds germinated, the young trees were allowed to grow for two years or more before being pulled for planting. When a tree that was grown for two years from seed was pulled from the ground and then packed for planting it was designated 2-0. The first number represents the number of years a tree is grown from seed in a nursery bed. The second number is the number of years the tree spent in a transplant bed. A tree that was grown for two years and then transplanted for an additional year would be designated as 2-1. This would provide a larger more robust seedling for the forester to select for use in more challenging growing conditions. A forester would be able to order, for example, Douglas-fir seedlings from an elevation of thirty-five hundred feet that were three years old, or 2-1 and have those planted in the target clear-cut. The 2-1 stock would be more expensive, of course, since it needed to be individually handled during the transplant operation. The resultant higher survival and success rate of the planted seedlings often made the extra expense worthwhile.

All of this work started with the identification of the specific individual trees that would provide healthy seed stock. In the parlance of the agency, this was called superior tree selection. I managed to get only one such contract in all my years in the business. This happened to be on the Cle Elum District of the Wenatchee National Forest a place I was beginning to know very well.

For this work I was obligated to wander the district and find a specified number of trees for a defined species list. These trees needed to be within a short distance of the road to provide easy access and make transporting the cones easier. The trees themselves had to exceed defined parameters of comparison to nearby and surrounding specimens of the same species and general age.

While the exact details and specifications are not of great importance to this discussion, the general idea was that I would find a nice stand of trees, ponderosa pine for example, and then pick the most impressive specimen in view. After visually identifying a likely candidate, I would measure that tree as well as the surrounding trees. In order to qualify, the chosen tree had to exhibit certain characteristics such as height, diameter, crown coverage and growth rate that exceeded the surrounding trees by a specified percentage. This ensured that the healthiest and heartiest specimen was selected.

I then trimmed the trunk of all branches to a height of sixteen feet in order to facilitate access for the climbers to follow. I painted a large orange band around the trunk at about five feet above the ground and tagged the tree with a sign designating it as a cone collection tree. I then charted it on a map for future reference.

When it was time for district personnel to collect cones for reforestation they would visit the selected trees identified by this work. The climbers would make the trip up and collect a batch of cones, which would eventually wind up in the nursery. Later, the trees grown from this seed would return to the district and be planted in nearby logged areas. This provided good, proven genetic stock to enhance the success rate of the replanting efforts.

From time to time, as the trees aged, this work would need to be redone in order to ensure an ongoing selection of superior trees to be used in the future. This is another interesting aspect of forestry that puts it in much the same category as other types of farming. In modern agriculture, selecting superior stock is commonly used to provide the strongest and best specimens in order to maximize production. It is from this perspective that one begins to understand why the Forest Service is assigned administration by the Department of Agriculture. Even though we may not think of farming as we drive through the forests of the Northwest, in truth growing trees and growing row crops are not so different. The details, of course, differ dramatically.

It's Wet in Quinault

The wettest place on earth is reported to be a location in the mountains of Colombia in South America that receives something like 525 inches of rain a year. In second place there is a bit of competition between a location in India and a spot on the Hawaiian Island of Kauai. They each get a reported average of about 460 inches of rain a year. Some years it's India and some years Hawaii that tops the chart. The wettest spot on the North American continent is reported to be Yakutat, Alaska with 160 inches a year although there seem to be a number of folks that feel that deep in the Olympic Peninsula are remote locations that top that amount by quite a bit. The truth is that the Alaskan coast may actually get more than Hawaii but there aren't the weather stations to measure it. The same is true with those out of the way Peninsula locations.

There is some discrepancy with recorded high rainfall totals from areas that come in just behind these "super wet" locations. Some information suggests that Mt Washington, New Hampshire tops the lower forty-eight states with 101 inches a year. However, records at the Quinault Ranger Station on the Olympic coast report just over 137 inches annually although this number does not appear in most "official" rainfall records for some reason. At some point, probably somewhere around 100 inches a year, I doubt it really matters very much what the actual number is. When that much rain is falling, you are simply assured you are going to get wet.

Close to the Quinault station is the village of Quillayute, which records just a drop or two over 101 inches yearly. This small community on the Washington coast is very near the location where Spanish explorers and Quinault Indians ran into conflict, an incident I referred to earlier in this book.

Quinault was also essentially where I landed my first contract on the Olympic National Forest. At the time, I knew it rained there, but even my years along the very wet Stillaguamish River Valley did not prepare me for what I found.

The contract was to do what I did best and most frequently – timber stand exams. The trees were all familiar to me, the same species I encountered routinely on the west side of the Cascades. My expectations were that I'd simply apply what I knew from past experience to this new area. After all, it was not far away from my home turf. There was just one range of mountains between my more familiar terrain and this magnificent forest overlooking the Pacific Ocean. Both were lowland temperate rain forests that started at the ocean and made their way up to the peaks.

It took only the first set of plots turned in to the district inspector to learn my first lesson about this new region. I worked a couple of days and provided about twenty survey samples for examination. While this was happening, I continued to move ahead and completed many more even though I was discovering some very large trees in these stands, which slowed progress somewhat. To measure these giants took longer than normal because I had to be further away from them to see the tops so I could shoot the heights with my optical inclinometer. Using trigonometry, I would measure the distance from a tree and then read the angle and calibrated height from a dial in the sighting lens of the inclinometer. Having to travel further from each tree slowed me down. However I was making up time by not having to drill every tree with my increment borer to establish the age since nearly all of the trees were three feet and larger in diameter. Some were much larger. I had drilled hundreds, maybe thousands of these trees with my hand increment borer. All these trees were of the same familiar species I had encountered before, and from history I knew that they would consistently be several hundred years old. The stand exam forms I filled out broke ages into groups with the real old growth being anything over two hundred and fifty years. These were giants, and were clearly older than that and so I entered them all in the plus 250 category. With no boring needed, I was still making good time even considering the height measurement slowdown. Then I received the results of my first inspection.

Every one of my plots failed. And every one of them failed for the same reason – the ages were off. For the big trees that I had estimated rather than drilled, the Forest Service inspector called me on every one of them. I had a brief discussion with the guy and was more than a little miffed at his obvious lack of skill. I knew that my experience was solid and that my numbers were correct, but he got the final call so I eventually just shut my mouth, took back all my survey cards and left, grumbling because this was going to seriously slow down my payment for work completed. The inspector's parting words were

"You need to drill those trees." And so I did.

Shocked? Absolutely. The first "old-growth" hemlock I tapped into required the full eighteen inches of my increment borer slide to hit the center. When I counted the rings, I could not believe what I saw. I counted them again. This three foot diameter tree was not fifty years old. I was stunned. I drilled a few more and had to admit, I was going to owe this inspector an apology. These stands in the lowlands had all been logged and this was the Olympic Peninsula's version of second growth. It turns out that the combination of low elevation; mild winter temperatures and the abundant rainfall create a tree-growing paradise unlike anything I had ever seen.

In addition to having to re-learn my concept of eyeball age estimating, I got to learn about rainfall. I was completely unprepared for just how much and how hard it rained along the coast. My seasons on the west side of the Cascades did not prepare me for the volume of water that drops here. Even though the amount of rain and the length of time it rained were far higher than anything I'd ever encountered – it was actually higher than anything I could even imagine – at some point it no longer matters. You can only get so wet. Your boots can only hold so much water and when it starts squishing out the tops because there is so much, it really does not make a difference whether you are living in the relatively "dry" climate of the Cascades or the seriously wet climate of the Olympics.

The Bear

The Olympic Peninsula. This is the most northwestern land in the continental United States. Even today, it is still isolated by Lower 48 standards. Roads surround it with U.S. highway 101 encircling it on three sides, but even with this loop of a road around the perimeter, there is no direct way across this mountainous region except by foot. Or by flying. Light plane pilots tend to avoid traveling over the center of the area because of the wildness of the National Park located there and because of the problems that a forced landing would cause. Having flown often over the Cascades, following one of the highways that provide trans-mountain ground passage, I always feel relatively confident that a forced landing could be effected within a reasonable distance of a highway or at least a logging road, and that it could be completed with some hope of success. This outcome is not so likely on the Peninsula.

From my earliest arrival in the Northwest I had been drawn to this remote area and had made the car trip around the Peninsula several times. My foot ventures had been extremely short and always by way of trails that were never more than a mile or two from the road. Because of my limited exploration of the area, I was somewhat unfamiliar with the details of the terrain. I had, however, been working in the woods in the Cascades of Washington and Oregon for six years by the time I arrived for my first taste of life in the Olympic Mountains.

My trusty partner Dan had followed me once again on a contract job with the Forest Service, this time to examine stands of timber that ranged in age from about ten years up through old growth. It was in one of these younger stands of replanted second growth that we found ourselves one day.

Even if someone takes the time to try and describe to you in detail, it's hard to fully comprehend what things are like off the road in the western reaches of the Olympic Peninsula. To say that it rains here is a ridiculous understatement. It rains here most of the time. Although there are times in the summer when you may get a week or two of good weather, this was not the case the summer that I was here. The result of all this moisture and of the relatively mild climate that exists in proximity to the ocean is one of extreme vegetative growth. Let me put it another way; it's a jungle out there. Move this terrain a few degrees to the south and you'd expect to see toucans and monkeys in the trees. This nearly impassable tangle of growth must be experienced to be fully understood.

Anyone who has traveled in the Northwest has seen the dense underbrush alongside the roads, assuming of course that the traveler ventured off the freeway or away from the strip-mall development. I spent several years of forestry work negotiating my way through these vine maple and thorny devils club infested areas in search of timber. I crawled up many a hillside where the vine maple was so dense and tall that I could not quite make out the trees above my head. I battled my way uphill through head high and higher huckleberry patches that always leaned downhill while I invariably needed to go the other direction. In all cases, my determination had prevailed and although I often spent long minutes extracting devils club thorns from my hands, and various other places, I always managed to get to where I was headed. Then, for the first time, I was immersed in the wetness that defines the Olympic Mountains.

I recall stepping into a second-growth stand of about ten years of age and walking no more than five feet into the brushy tangle before I came up against a wall. A wall, that is, of the branches of cascara trees. The cascara is a hardwood that grows throughout the Northwest, reaching small tree size at best. An herbal laxative extract is made from the bark. This young stand of second growth had been taken over by an aggressive group of these trees that were about five to ten feet tall. It happens that the young deciduous cascara tree begins branching about a foot or so off the ground and sends out additional lateral branches at about one foot intervals. This usually presents little problem because the trees are not typically found in more than ones or twos. This stand was decidedly different. This was a veritable cascara plantation. Unable to move forward through the tangle of branches, I moved to one side and attempted to work my way through. Again, I was stopped against a wall of interwoven branches. With the base of the trees only a few feet apart, the branches wove a fence that started at ground level and extended to head high. I tried again and was blocked again. I got down on my stomach and attempted to crawl underneath; believing that the clump was only one or two trees deep and I could break through on the other side. I was trapped on my belly, squirming under the trees as though I were a soldier in the fields of France crawling under concertina wire trying to get through to the enemy lines. I never did make it. I backed out and made my way back to the truck on the road, not two hundred feet away. There stood Dan. Grinning.

"You couldn't squeeze a weasel through that could you?" he said. We never did finish that timber stand exam, telling the Forest Service that it was inaccessible. I don't know what they thought. Keep in mind this physical description as I return to the tale at hand.

While my current location did not entirely rival the density of the cascara plantation, it was still incredibly dense with the brush typical of what was found in the region. It additionally offered a lovely plant known as the evergreen blackberry, a species of the tasty fruit-bearing bush that is particularly hardy due mostly to its inch thick stems that like growing horizontally. The fat stems contained large sized thorns that inflicted memorable wounds on the unwary. Due to the thickness of the brush, both Dan and I were forced from time to time to revert to the "crawlin' on our bellies like a reptile" mode of travel in order to maintain a reasonably straight transect line as we surveyed the contents of this southeast facing slope.

We were doing our usual cross slope travel, following parallel lines about three hundred feet apart when I began smelling a foul odor. The aroma was of rotting fish. I looked to the bottom of the hill where the clear-cut area gave way to the timbered bottom. I saw no river or stream down there, but given the quantify of rain in the area, every ravine, draw and low spot had some sort of water moving through it so

I supposed the smell might be related to that. The aroma came and went as I continued on my way, walking, climbing over logs, crawling under and through the blackberries, thoroughly wet from the drizzle, cold, and all the while examining my motives for doing this type of work.

I continued to wonder about the odor as I moved. It had become stronger and seemed to hang in the air, not fading in and out as before. As I rose after crawling under a downed log, I heard a tremendous commotion of something crashing in the brush below me, followed in just moments by a sudden blur of dark motion and then - whoosh - past me raced a medium-sized black bear on a mission to get to the top of the hill in as short a time as possible. The bear passed directly in front of me, maybe five feet away, with not so much as a glance in my direction as it crashed through the impossible tangle of undergrowth. I don't think the bear even knew I was there. It happened so suddenly, so unexpectedly, that I never began to think of danger or fear or other bear-related emotions. Mostly I was just surprised.

The smell that had been hanging in the air was obviously from the bear. That much was clear as it fled uphill past me, leaving in its wake a sickly, rotting aroma. Whatever that critter had eaten for lunch did not smell appetizing. I continued on my line of travel as I heard the bear break out of the brush above me, probably onto the road that ran parallel to us. I could hear it continuing uphill as it went on its way. In a few minutes, I reached the timber on the opposite end of the young stand of trees and broke into relatively clear terrain on the old fire trail that had been cut alongside the clear-cut, providing a holding line for the crew that burned the slash left after the loggers departed. I followed this line down the hill to intercept Dan where he and I would continue downhill to the next line of travel and begin the return trip for our next transect of the survey. As I neared Dan, standing on a stump, I could see a grin.

"Imagine my surprise," he bellowed at me as I came into view, "when, crawling on my belly through the brush, I looked up and into the eyes of a bear! Not two feet away from me mind you! There was no way I could get away. I was pinned to the ground. The bear looked at me. I looked at him. I don't know whose eyes were the biggest."

"So did he eat you?" I asked.

"He woofed at me and left in such a hurry that he even kicked dirt in my face," Dan said laughing. I guess if I encountered Dan crawling on his belly through the wet underbrush of an Olympic Mountain morning, then I, in the manner of the bear, would have run for my life as well.

Contract Planting Round Two

I started out the next season with what was becoming my standard activity – tree planting. I managed to get two big contracts that year, one for Scott Paper and one for the Forest Service. The Scott contract let me reassemble more or less the same crew I had had the year before. This time we had the advantage of experience and we moved quickly through the work and everyone made out handsomely. I did lose my best man when the folks from Scott approached me about offering him a permanent position with them. They obviously saw just how hard he worked and how good he was, so when we finished the contract I had to bid him goodbye. It was a much better arrangement for him, obviously, so even though it cost me my strongest planter, there was some personal satisfaction in seeing a deserving guy get a break.

I followed up with a Forest Service contract on, for me, a new district. We traveled north along the Skagit River and worked on the Mount Baker Ranger District for a couple of months in bad weather and challenging terrain. This was the first time I acted only as the contractor and did not do any of the planting myself. After a couple of weeks of operating only as a foreman, monitoring progress, explaining plans for covering the area and being the mule that carried new bags of trees into the clear-cut for the planters, I needed to move on to look into another contract I was trying to land. I placed one of my longer term planters in charge, a bit of mistake as it later turned out, when he made a few bad decisions that ended up costing me both time and money. I returned to the job site in time to get things done on schedule.

As that work was winding down, I found myself with yet another adventure looming with a timber stand exam contract on the Umatilla National Forest is southeastern Washington. This was yet another area I had never visited.

With only a couple of days remaining to wrap up the Forest Service planting project, I loaded up my truck with my work gear and camping supplies and said goodbye to the planting crew, and headed east over the Cascades to see what sort of country awaited me.

The Blue Mountains

Washington is a land of dramatic contrast. Along the Pacific Coast, valleys such as that of the Hoh River receive something like one hundred and sixty inches of rain a year. There are places near Mt Olympus that reportedly receive more like two hundred inches. Although there is inconsistency in the actual rainfall totals reported depending on which source one sites, it is without disagreement that on the east side of the Cascades annual precipitation of less ten inches can be found in many locations. The differences between the eastern and western part of the state are striking because of this. At times, when you are in the Puget Sound lowlands and the weather is bad with low visibilities, you would never suspect that much more than hills could surround you as you travel over the rolling landscape. Let the sun appear with clear skies and you'll note that you were wrong as you stare at the fourteen thousand foot bulk of Mt. Rainier.

I've traveled the rocky northwest coastline with its rugged ocean fronting cliffs and steep timbered slopes. I have seen the long sandy beaches that line the Pacific just north of the Columbia River, climbed high on the glaciers of Mt. Baker and Mt. Rainer and have walked and driven through the desert sage of the central interior. I had traveled extensively through the Northeast corner of the state above Spokane where the Rocky Mountains edge their way across the state line from Idaho and have visited the spot where the Snake River empties into the

Columbia. As I traveled for the first time through the undulating Palouse prairies that led me toward the southeast corner of the state, I marveled at the multi-colored shimmering wheat that absolutely glowed in the lowering sun of a June evening. That was where I found myself on my way to the last, for me, unexplored corner of this marvelous Northwest country.

I arrived that first time, in the Blue Mountains, in the dark. It was a familiar experience for me, finding a quiet spot to get off the road and camp with no real idea where I was. Quiet is relative, of course, and by city standards I could easily have parked in the middle of the road and enjoyed a peaceful night. I would not likely be disturbed by anyone as I sat on a Forest Service road. That was a bit extreme even for me, however, so I settled for a small turnout that led to a clearing a couple of hundred feet from the road. I climbed into the back of my pickup, cooked a pot of ramen noodles with cheese and broccoli, drank a beer and settled into my sleeping bag, looking up through the branches of the trees at the stars overhead. It was absolutely quiet.

My first recollection of seeing anything other than the night sky in the Blues is still clear in my mind. I awoke before dawn to see rows of cirrus clouds glowing pink overhead. They moved slowly but perceptibly toward the east as they reflected the light of the still unseen sun. I remember hearing birds and lying quietly, watching the glowing clouds change from one deep shade of pink to another, then to orange and then gradually to glow into brilliant white. I sat up, took a look around to survey this new country and was surprised to see that everything around me was flat. Of course, I couldn't see far and had no real idea of what actually lay beyond the few hundred feet that I could see, but all indications were that I was not actually surrounded by mountains.

By mid-day, I was starting on the first of the many stand-exam plots that I would establish on the Pomeroy Ranger District of the Umatilla National Forest. It was becoming clear to me that this place was unlike anywhere else I had ever been. It seemed, somehow, upside down to me. This was because I had discovered that the roads I was traveling were on the ridge tops and the timber I would survey was found over the plateau edge dropping into the valleys below. I was very acclimatized to high mountain terrain such as is found in the Olympics and the Cascades. There, the roads begin in the lowlands and force their way uphill into the mountains, fighting for every inch of altitude gain until they finally reach an elevation at which the timber is no longer harvestable. At that point, it is because either the ground is too steep and rocky or the size of the trees becomes less appealing to the loggers. At about five thousand feet in the Cascades, trees are beginning to struggle for their lives. Thin soil and severe climate makes it a tough place to do business if you're a tree at that altitude. The topography of these areas had led me to finding most of my work beginning at a road and heading uphill. Suddenly, in the Blues, the exact opposite was true as I found all my trips began the day from a hilltop road and then heading downhill into the trees.

Much of the country in the region consists of flat topped mountains, not quite mesa-like but with distinct level highlands and steep heavily timbered slopes descending down into the river and stream bottoms. The majority of the timber is to be found on these slopes so I would have drop into these slopes to survey the timber. Every trip down, of course, comes with the price of the return trip up and out.

On the gently sloping "mesa" tops, I found large stands of lodgepole pine, all of about the same size and age, due apparently to a ravaging fire that swept through the region about fifty years before I showed up. It was a beautiful place, these top-forests, with very little brush, quite unlike the dense rainforest growth of the western regions, and gentle slopes that made walking easy and inviting. Each time I reached the edge of one of these flat mountains, I would be rewarded with long views in whatever direction I happened to be traveling.

After a couple of days in what seemed near-perfect conditions, things took a decided turn in the down direction as the weather deteriorated. The dry climate I was accustomed to east of the Cascades seemed to not apply at this distant eastern boundary of the state. The east bound weather systems had regained some moisture after having traveled across the dry interior of the state. I spent a good two weeks living in the back of my pickup with the rain fly from my tent rigged over the truck bed since I didn't have a canopy on the rig. The rain fly fit snugly along the sides and back so I was well protected both from the wind and the rain, but after the first twenty-four hours everything I had was wet and it stayed that way until I finally left the area when I gave up and fled because the rain would not. A great many of my memories of working in the woods of the Northwest involve memories of the wet. This place and this time rather sum up that experience. And it wasn't just wet. At almost five thousand feet, it was cold even though it was late June.

If you're living in St. Louis or Washington D.C. or even Chicago it may be hard to imagine what it's like at that altitude and in the Northwest mountains in summer when weather such as that arrives. It's not usually quite cold enough to snow, although it very well might, but neither is it warm enough that you could possibly get through the day without gloves. Forty degrees, twenty knots of gusty wind, and absolutely continual rain. It's raining when you wake in the morning. It's raining every time you wake at night. It rains all day long as you walk in your rubber rain gear, water dripping into your eyes and down the collar of your jacket, chilling your neck and back and managing to wet you all the way to your underwear. Socks are always absolutely squishy in spite of the amount of oil rubbed into your boots. Under my rain jacket I wore my cruisers vest with the pockets stuffed with pencils and plastic flagging, compass, altimeter, relaskope and prisms, notebooks, maps and aerial photos. Increment borers and diameter tapes had to be rinsed daily in WD40 to inhibit rust since they were constantly wet. Even the writes-in-the-rain paper becomes so damp that corrections have to be penciled in for changing once the page is dried. This was the kind of weather that drove me into town.

In such conditions, at least a couple of times a week I would break down and have to return to civilization. I would need to see an electric light and watch some television. But mostly I would need to dry myself out a bit in order to face the next morning. So, I'd visit whatever bar happened to be open and nearby, order the fried chicken and jo-jos and drink a glass or two of beer as I took on food and stared at whatever happened to be showing on the television in the bar.

Appearing as I did, out of the wet and dark, I would usually manage to strike up a conversation with some local who chose to spend his evening the same as me although usually for different reasons. From these people I would learn a bit about local activities and politics and other such information. From these conversations it became clear that most places seem to be a lot like every other place I'd been. Concerns may have varied a bit from town to town but usually it was because one area was more of a ranching and farming community than a logging one. This meant the issues were beef and wheat prices instead of what I viewed as the more usual concerns over stumpage prices for fir and cedar. In the Blues the complaints were that the government was killing them with increased grazing fees and raising hell with the latest involvement over price controls. I found the same problems for these people as I had seen on the logging communities of the Cascades. The same complaints about government regulations and meddling seemed to pepper the conversations in all places, with only the specifics of the regional topics differing. All in all, it was just people trying to understand what the world was doing to them and trying to make a living. In that regard, they were exactly the same as me.

Eventually, though, it would get late enough and I would be dry enough to head back into the hills and back to the quiet of my truck bed. Midway through the summer, things took a decided turn for the better. I finished up a portion of the contract, went home to visit my wife and kids and bought myself a trailer. No more sleeping in a pickup bed for this boy.

The Fleetwood was a 1953, teardrop trailer with a single back bunk, a sink with a manual pump and a ten gallon holding tank. It had a two burner propane stove and an oven. It had a table that would seat four, if they were small and good friends, and it had a small closet. A tiny icebox would hold a bag of ice, a head of lettuce and about two six packs of beer. The table would break down and provide sleeping for half of the aforementioned close-knit group. It was a beauty, a classic, and for six-hundred dollars, a real bargain. I always figured that the real measure of value was that I paid about ten cents a pound for this trailer because it sure seemed like it weighed about six thousand pounds. At maybe fifteen feet long, it's hard for the modern trailer-tower to relate to this statement, but I think in the days in which this beast was built and launched, the manufacturer used real wood throughout. Unlike today's trailer of small framing lumber and lots of aluminum and plastic, the 'Wood was built like a house using two by fours and larger over a steel frame. She was built to last. That's why at nearly forty years old these rigs were at the time still intact and being dragged all over the country.

The 'Wood was to accompany the Island Forestry Experience from that point onward. Everywhere we went, the Fleetwood would get dragged along. It was corporate headquarters, the cook house, the crew house, the guest house, the field office and one night following an intense spell of drinking, it even became the company jet as Dan and I pretended to pilot the beast home, fleeing in our intoxicated silliness, from the pounding rain that threatened to float us away. The 'Wood, on her maiden voyage, came back to the Blue Mountains with me.

At this point, I was rather well acquainted with the area in which I was working, and I had already selected my base location as I drove across the state. At a point just along the Washington - Oregon border, looking east and seeing Idaho, the Blue Mountains drop steeply away to the south into the valley of the Grande Ronde River. At this summit point, a road travels east to west and provides dramatic long-distance views south to the High Wallowa Mountains down in Oregon. The Forest Service, recognizing the value of this vista, established a Guard Station on this road, using the commanding view as a prime location for a fire lookout. From the front porch of the Wenatchee Guard Station, the lookout can survey hundreds of square miles of timber and rangeland while sitting in his rocker, without the common necessity of climbing into a twelve by twelve tower as is usual in the lookout profession. Just up the road to the west, I settled the Fleetwood into a road side turnout that provided me with one of the most dramatic views I was to have in all my years of working outside. This premier site included easy road-frontage access, truly spectacular views, and less than one-quarter mile away was a lovely spring that was established to provide water for grazing stock by draining into a tank. What could be finer? All that was lacking was electricity and I would have had all of the comforts of home. That was what I was thinking as I sat on my lawn chair one evening enjoying a fresh salad and dinner from my gourmet kitchen when I heard the distant buzz of a small engine. Chainsaw? No. Too regular. Lawnmower? Don't be ridiculous. Generator? Had to be. Electricity. Damn. Watch out what you ask for, as the saying goes.

A short stroll back up the road to the Wenatchee Guard Station and I found the source of the noise. It was a generator, all right, and it was connected to a television. The resident guard, it turns out, was a football fan, and it being late August and a Monday night he intended to watch the NFL. For the next three weeks while I finished up my contract on the district, I spent each Monday evening with the Forest Service lookout drinking beer, munching pizza, and watching Monday Night Football. And all of this came with a view that had to be seen to be believed.

This period was as marked a contrast with my June experience here as was possible. Following the televised game , I would walk the half mile back down the road in the dark, listening to coyotes howl and yip down the canyon to the south and up the ridge to the West into the Tucannon Wilderness and imagine how it would be that life could get any better than this.

Moments

Sometimes during my years in the outdoors, there were moments that were simply remarkable. These were moments that were notable both for their simplicity and for their beauty. It might be a view that opened up as I crested a ridge. Other times it was a dramatic sunrise or sunset. There were thunderstorms and beautiful blue sky days and even the quiet and peace of a low cloud drizzle that left me feeling lucky to have the experience.

One such miracle was the day I was doing stand exams on the Pomeroy Ranger District of the Umatilla National Forest near Walla Walla. It was a middle time: the middle of July and the middle of the week and the middle of the day. It was scorching hot with neither wind nor clouds. The heat cooked the pine trees to the point that I could smell the resin in the air as I walked through the land of bare and nearly flat ridge tops that looked down into the deeply forested, steep-walled canyons.

I had stopped in the shade of the ponderosa pines that bordered a small stream so I could take a break for lunch while I sat in the slightly cooler air and rested for a bit. I had just un-wrapped a sandwich and taken my first bite when I heard a noise on the other side of the stream. I looked toward the sound but saw nothing at first. With my ears on alert, I sat quietly eating, looking and waiting. Moments later an elk appeared at the edge of the clearing above and looked my way. I sat in the deep shade at the base of a good sized pine with the washed out sun-blazed brilliant blue sky at my back. Had I been standing where the elk was and looking at where I sat, I could have only seen a black shadow against the skyline. The sun and sky were so bright that the shadows along the stream at the base of the trees were dark and deep. The elk, looking directly at me, apparently could not see me.

I sat mid-bite, breathless, my sandwich held halfway to my mouth. The elk showed no sign of seeing me so I concluded that as long as I remained still I was fairly invisible even though the animal was sniffing the air. She knew something was in the area but could not make me out against the dark background. As I watched, another elk appeared. This one showed no sign of seeing me either and the two of them slowly stepped their way down the hill to the edge of the stream where they drank, then looked up and around, then drank again. Both animals jumped slightly at a sound behind them and turned together to look at yet another elk just stepping into sight. And then another and another and another. I finally counted twelve cow elk when the migration seemed to be over. All of them stood along the bank of the stream, quietly drinking, some no more than twenty feet from me and not one showing the slightest indication that they were aware of my presence. Or maybe they just didn't care.

For probably ten minutes I sat still, although time seemed to not exist, remaining as motionless as I could, breathing as little as possible. I moved only my eyes and imagined moving my ears in the way I saw them doing, trying to catch the same sounds that they seemed to hear.

Finally, their thirst dealt with, they began to slip away by ones and twos, back up the slight rise over which they had appeared. In moments they were gone and I was not quite certain I had actually seen them. I resumed eating my lunch, smiling, and taking a bit more note of the biting smell of the pine air; listening a bit more intently at the sounds in the air, and marveling at how lucky I was to be sitting there.

The Mountains of Idaho

I don't know any longer what exactly I expected the first time I arrived here. For years I carried mental images of this part of the world and as is often the case when you spend a lot of time in anticipation of something, the reality and the expectation never quite meet. In fact what I found was both much less and much more than I expected.

One thing can be said about central Idaho. It's a long way from anywhere else to there. A particular characteristic that accompanies a far-away place is that the roads are likely to be a bit less elegant than what one finds in a more populous area. For obvious reasons, road access in the area I was heading to was much less agreeable than what I was familiar with in my home area of the planet. My routine complaint to nearly anyone who will listen is that there are just too many people and too many cars on too few roads. If we had either fewer people or fewer cars or a few more and larger roads then things would be not so bad, or so goes the argument. In fact it seems that road capacity, like personal financial budgets, will always expand to utilize completely whatever resource is available. By the time I reached the approaches to Grangeville, however, the memories of multi-lane freeways and traffic were fading fast. There were certainly no crowds here, but still it takes a lot longer to reach the objective in this country, simply because the roads are not designed for speed.

I drove to Grangeville and then continued to Elk City to meet with Forest Service personnel for a contract I had won that would be located near the Red River Ranger Station, which was even more remote than either of the two towns I had already passed through. Today the Red River station, like so many other small ones around the West, has closed and the administrative duties have merged with the Elk City District. It remains one of the more remote spots in the country.

The area managed by the Elk City and Red River group borders the Selway-Bitterroot Wilderness. Outside of Alaska, this is the third largest wilderness area in the U.S. The fact that just south of the Selway-Bitterroot is the second largest wilderness in the continental U.S. – The Frank Church Wilderness - means there is a lot of very wild country in this area. The stand of timber I was to be looking at was butted up against the western boundary of these 3.7 million acres of wild land.

I arrived in Elk City on the first day of July, ready to start work on a timber stand exam that would cover about six-thousand acres of high country old-growth timber. That is a lot of ground to look at, and although I was completely unfamiliar with the terrain and with the timber types, I was confident that with my experience I would soon pick up what information I needed to make this job a profitable experience. And why not since I felt myself a quick study and had shown on several other occasions that I could learn what I needed on the job. It turned out that while I was easily able to learn to distinguish the new plants I encountered, I was less able to deal with the personalities that I met.

Dan and I had dragged the trusty Fleetwood trailer across Washington and into these remote mountains to use it as our home while doing this work. Upon arriving at the Red River Ranger Station we dropped the trailer off with a friend I had met in Oregon while I was stationed there. He had recently made the transfer from the Blue River District in Oregon to the Red River District in Idaho, a fact that gave us no end of pleasure in discussing place names over beers. Leaving the trailer that first night seemed a good idea while we scoped out the work area, being completely unfamiliar with the locale. The roads turned out to be very long and very bad. The distance between the last imaginable parking spot for the trailer and the trailhead that provided access to the six thousand acres was simply too far to be practical. In addition, it turned out that just to access the near corner of the timber stand would be a two-mile hike over an abandoned road that finally turned into trail. I had not figured on that since the maps I had reviewed showed road access all the way in. That was my first mistake. Once we hiked in and got to the southern boundary of the timber and I was able to look at our objective, it was nearly overwhelming.

I had done stand exams prior to this that measured in the thousands of acres. Typically, however, they were composed of multiple stands of timber in separate locations so I would do a couple of hundred acres here, a couple of hundred there and so forth. I would drive or hike into these areas, work them for a few days and then move on. Arriving at the corner of a contiguous six thousand acres, I was stopped in my tracks. Seeing it all in one piece, all in one parcel, was daunting. I looked to the north at distant peaks. Then I looked east and across a gently sloping bowl that was surrounded by a horseshoe shaped ridge. We stood in the closed circle of the horseshoe with the east and west ridgelines running to the north of us and forming the two sides of the horseshoe. It was miles to the far end. One square mile covers six hundred acres. This one was ten times that size.

I immediately sensed the difficulty we were to face here. The long road access in, the hike just to get to the entry side of the stand, and worst of all, the incredible distances we would need to cover to put plots in place across this ten square mile basin.

For starters, we decided we would leave the trailer at the bottom of the road, along the river there, and drive the several miles of bad road to the trailhead. We planned to carry in camping gear and stay two nights on site, working daylight to dark. Every third day we would come out, take a break and resupply. It seemed a reasonable enough plan.

The first day we lugged all our gear in, found a nice flat spot with a view of the vast wilderness and set up camp. We then made plans for how we were going to complete our plots. We determined that the most efficient method would be to make long east to west transects starting from our camp on the west ridgeline, dropping down into the basin and then back up to the east ridgeline on the far side. Assuming we were able to make reasonable speed, we would always end the day on one or the other of these ridges, which both had primitive game trails worn into them that would provide us reasonable access back to camp or back to the entry trail. By running these plot lines across the basin, we would do a series of ever-farther trips to the north as we gradually made our way back and forth across the horseshoe until we reached the open end and finished our work.

The first day it snowed. It was July 4th. There was so much snow on the ground we were unable to work since we would need to be able to identify plants on the ground as part of the work. That's hard to do when you cannot see them. We made our way back out, drove down the snow covered road to the trailer and settled in. It took a couple of days for things to melt out and back we went, hopeful of better results.

Our first actual work day found us making the initial transect line headed east across the basin from near our camp. At least by this time we were feeling more comfortable, back to doing things we knew. Having worked together many times before, we applied our usual practice of setting up parallel lines, each of us doing a series of plots spaced a predetermined distance apart. We moved much more slowly than usual, impeded by the need to look up a few new plants in our field guidebooks and we spent a fair amount of time shouting back and forth through the trees. We were only a few hundred feet apart so this was not too problematic. What did present difficulties, however, was what we encountered as we neared the bottom of the basin. Located in the lower regions we found enormous thickets of yew trees. These nearly impenetrable thickets were unlike anything I had ever seen. Several hundred years old, and much taller and denser than any I had ever before encountered, they are a favored habitat of moose. I did not know that at the time, but soon figured it out while we were trying to navigate through and around these dense growths and started seeing moose tracks everywhere.

Taking one problem at a time, Dan and I determined we would have to modify our between-plot pacing to accommodate the frequent side trips around these thickets. As described earlier, we measured the distance between plots by pacing. When encountering a wall of yew, we had little choice but to flag the route to the point at which we hit this dead-end, make a detour to one side or the other, find our way around it and return to the approximate location relative to a straight line as indicated by the flag line we had left on our way in. The surveyors tape left hanging along our route of travel enabled the Forest Service inspectors to locate our plots for review. The problem we now faced was that once on the other side of the thicket, we could not always see the flag line. A close approximation was the best we could do. This was not a concern to me given the considerable experience we both had in doing these exams. We were confident we would be "close enough for government work" in locating the plot centers, so we continued on our way.

This worked out fine for us. But it was not adequate for the government inspectors. When the pair of them arrived a couple of days later, I turned over the results of our first two days of work. We had picked up speed a bit by then, but it was still much slower going than I had expected and was taking us longer than any stand exams I had ever done anywhere, even though the trees were much smaller than the big west side giants of the Cascades. The terrain and the brush and the thickets of yew and the distances were the culprits. The results of the first inspection were similar to the results of my first stand exam inspection on the Olympic Peninsula. Every one of our plots failed.

I reconnected with the inspection team the next day and was surprised to learn that they were working as a pair when doing the inspections and were using a tape measure to locate the plots. They failed us if we were outside a narrow tolerance of that measure, and given the fact that we were pacing and making multiple detours around yew thickets on every plot line, it really was not a surprise. If we were supposed to be five hundred feet apart and came in at four hundred and seventy-five, we failed. I could not believe it. With the time it would take to measure, physically, the distance between each plot, calculating for slope and forcing our way through the yew thickets, it would have been possible to complete only eight or ten plots on a good day with both of us working. My target was closer to thirty in order for us to make any kind of reasonable income and to complete on time. This work was bid based on past experience. Under their definition of the terms, my bid should have been three times as much or more, but as the low bidder I won. It should be noted that I did not win by much so anyone else trying to do this work would have faced the same issue. I mentioned difficult personalities earlier. There was no give in these guys. It felt like they wanted to punish us for daring to come from so far away to do this work and many comments were made that were clearly intended to let me know how "you boys out on the coast don't understand our country here". It was a disaster.

On the plus side were three things that made this ill-fated trip a fabulous experience in spite of these problems. First was the chance to visit with my old friend, Paul, from Oregon. We spent several evenings on the Red River compound and barbequed and played guitar and drank beer while enjoying the Idaho summer.

Second was the excitement of seeing so many moose while we were there. The initial moose encounter was the first night Dan and I spent in our tent on the job site, just before the snow fell. We were awakened late in the night, or early in the morning, I don't know which, by a tremendous crashing and stomping just outside the tent. We had no idea what was marauding out there but neither of us were anxious to find out. We huddled quietly in the tent, not daring to open the flap and eventually the unknown intruder left. In the morning, we found a parade of moose tracks surrounding the tent. Given what I know now about moose and how dangerous they are, I can only conclude that our naivety may have saved us. Another night while we were camped streamside in the Fleetwood trailer, I was awakened by what sounded like a pig snorting outside the window. I looked out and in the moonlight, standing belly deep in the river, was a large bull moose slurping up great gulps of aquatic plants and making all sorts of noise. Over the coming days we saw more of these great beasts both in the woods and in the rivers.

And the third great pleasure was the day Dan and I took off, despondent from the impossibility of satisfying the Forest Service inspectors. We loaded a cooler full of ice and beer in the truck and headed south on the gravel road to the tiny hamlet of Dixie. You can find this community on the map, but only because there is absolutely nothing else anywhere near it. South of the Red River Ranger Station, Dixie is still the "end of the road" in this part of the world. There were logging roads we followed even beyond Dixie until we came to a trailhead that led down and into the Salmon River canyon. We lugged our cooler and two lawn chairs down the trail, ending up about four thousand feet lower than where we had been working, sitting in hundred degree heat literally in the middle of nowhere. As we sat there, raft loads of travelers floated by. I could tell by their expressions they were baffled by our presence. By the time they passed our location, they had likely been on the river three or four days. Seeing the lawn chairs and the cooler and no visible means of access to what was a genuinely remote location must have made them wonder who the beer drinking lunatics were that they saw sitting alongside that wilderness river.

Ultimately, I gave up on this contract. After repeated attempts to work things out and convince the local Forest Service folks that we could provide meaningful data doing the work in a more aggressive fashion, I decided it was simply not worth the cost and the effort to continue. As much as I hated walking away with the job undone, there were other opportunities awaiting us that would allow us to utilize our skills and make some money at the same time.

By mid-July, we bade Idaho farewell and headed back west to take on a stand exam contract on familiar territory – the Wenatchee National Forest. Smaller by several thousand acres, this job came with its own set of problems, mostly due to access difficulties not unlike what we were leaving. In fact, to get to the timber on the Wenatchee we spent most of the summer swimming and wading the Wenatchee River. While that project went well and the inspection team on that district seemed to find our work more than satisfactory, there was one little problem at the end.

The River

Picture this: It is late October and late in the day; just before sunset along the eastern slopes of the Cascade Mountains. There is a little nip of fall in the air and the mountainsides are ablaze in reds and yellows. I have my daypack on my back. My boots are tied together by the laces and hung around my neck. This is my last trip across the river on this contract job of cruising timber for the Forest Service.

Since mid-summer I had been making this twice-daily river crossing between my camp on the road side of the river and the heavily timbered slopes on the other side of the water. I had completed one hundred and thirteen successful river crossings and had one more to go. Midway across on this very last trip, I lost my footing and fell in.

I remember feeling annoyed with myself as I bounced along the river bed, gradually moved down river by the current. I was annoyed that all my tools and the maps and notes that were in my backpack were getting wet. Annoyed.

I became concerned when I tried to stop myself from bouncing along downstream and discovered I could not. My first sensation of fear came when I realized I could not stand up even had I been able to stop myself in the current. I could not stand since my chest waders - did I mention that I was wearing chest waders - were full of water. One gallon of water weighs eight pounds. I had ten or fifteen gallons aboard.

I was too heavy to stand but buoyant enough for the river to keep me moving right along. In no time at all I bounced my way downstream into a deeper pool and I was underwater, looking up at the fading daylight. I remember being immediately worried for the new Seiko digital watch my wife had given me a couple of weeks earlier for my birthday. I remember a pencil floating out of my pocket and in front of my face. I had this odd sensation of realizing I had my sunglasses on, my baseball cap on, and I was sitting on the bottom of a river in ten feet of water surrounded by huge boulders. And I was about to drown.

Funny things happen when you've got one foot in this life and one into whatever comes next. The clear part of my mind said, "You've got to do something now or you are going to die!" I jettisoned the boots and struggled to remove the backpack, but I couldn't get it off. The straps were wet and the pack was full of water. The straps for the waders were inaccessible under the backpack straps. I started crawling and scooting along the bottom, attempting to make my way to the edge of the river. It seemed a long time that I was down there although I know that it must not have been. The lack of oxygen was becoming a problem and I was just at that point of becoming someone else looking down on myself when I managed to get my head out of the water and breathe.

It was several minutes of sitting on top of a rock along the riverbank before I had the strength to do anything. Eventually I recharged enough to work my way out of the backpack, which I tossed to the bank. It hit hard and water poured from the seams. At that point, I was able to loosen the straps to the waders and work my way out of them while sitting half submerged. Soaked, exhausted and cold, I finally struggled to shore and again remained motionless for several minutes. I left the waders at that spot. Never again did I plan to step into another pair. It was only a short walk back to my camp and I made the trip in my soaking wet sneakers that I pulled from the now drained backpack. I salvaged all my work papers with minimal damage but the aerial photos were destroyed. I left the waders and lost my cork boots and a pencil, but my watch continued to work and I remained alive.

I spent a good part of that evening sitting around a campfire, enjoying the early fall night and feeling a bit more alive than I had the day before. I have been back to that spot a few times since and as I look at the shallow where I took the tumble, the water barely two feet deep, I wonder at the power of water in a river and wonder at the directions our lives take. And I wonder why sometimes there are happy endings and sometimes not. It obviously was not my time to go. I often remember just how close to the edge I came that day.

A New Season

Another season started with tree planting. Another season of working for private firms early – Scott Paper again and the Port Blakely Mill Company – and then the Forest Service as the higher elevation land opened up. With a slightly modified crew, I stayed busy for the early months while waiting to see what new work I could find. I was enjoying running crews less and less, tired of dealing with the logistics of fielding twenty person teams with saws and planting equipment. It was a lot of work to keep things repaired and getting more and more expensive. It was also difficult early in the season because until I began getting paid for our planting work I was forced to come up with wages for the crew in advance of getting invoices cleared by the Forest Service. I managed this mostly by a line of credit at my local bank. While the money was good from these large scale projects, the administrative activities were less and less interesting to me. I decided after this season I would concentrate solely on the more solitary work of wandering the timber doing stand exams. The money was just as good without the additional burdens, and there seemed to be a lot of contracts to bid on.

The only problem was, early in the year the only contracts I seemed to land were for planting. So, rather than field my own crew again, I ended up signing back on with the Forest Service for a short stint. For this posting, I was hired as a foreman for the planting crew on the Mt Baker Ranger District where I'd planted the spring before. I certainly knew the work, and I knew the terrain, so it worked out quite well although it seemed odd to be back on the other side of the Forest Service fence.

As spring progressed and the planting work was wrapping up, I was pressed into service for my favorite work. I took a partner with me every day since, unlike my own methods, it was considered by the Forest Service wise to not travel alone in the rugged mountainous terrain. Actually, this is very good advice, it just seemed that a good part of the time I would end up on my own when working contracts. I also applied much the same logic even while employed and would work with my partner running a parallel line. We could cover twice the ground and still be within shouting distance. That proved to be a useful fact on one particular day while working deep in the Cascade Mountains.

The Bears on Bacon Creek

The farther north you travel in the Cascades, the more rugged the country becomes. North of the Skagit River on the way toward the wilds of the Pickett Range, the timber is big and the land is steep. Much of this country is in wilderness and parks, thankfully, and as such is protected from logging and road building. The harvestable timber on the federal forest land extends right to these wilderness boundaries, however, and the roads go to those boundaries as well. Bacon Creek runs south out of this glacier covered and rock strewn world, the stream as wild as it ever was except for the lower reaches, where gravel logging roads follow it for a few miles. The creek empties into the Skagit River just above the mountain town of Marblemount and below the Seattle City Light town of Newhalem.

I was looking at some timber for the Baker River Ranger District the time that Stan and I went to Bacon Creek. It was my first and remains my only visit to this beautiful spot. A road on the east side of the stream followed along the bank for a short distance before heading to the right and uphill, eventually dead-ending into a clear-cut. Across the water, on the west, the land sloped uphill steeply until it ended in bare rock and ice. A couple of thousand feet above the creek, a logging road penetrated almost to the protected North Cascades Park boundary. Above the road was a clear-cut, several years old. Below the road were the old-growth trees in the stand we were to examine for possible inclusion in a future timber sale. Our plan was to park one of our vehicles at the bottom along the stream on the road east of the river and drive the other to the end of the high road. We would then make a single survey line directly downhill, cross Bacon Creek, retrieve the first vehicle and drive back up for the other. Allowing gravity to work for us would make for a much easier trip through this stand of timber. Since we were not doing the work on contract, but as employees of the Forest Service, time was not an issue so the ferry plan would make for a series of relatively easy days.

Arriving at the starting point on the first morning, we drove to the end of the upper road and examined the terrain we were about to enter. The northern boundary of the timber, on our left side as we faced downhill, was marked by a steep ravine filled with roaring water aimed straight down toward Bacon Creek. This would make for an easy left side demarcation. We planned to make parallel survey lines down the hill. I would follow the ravine and Stan, my partner, would move about three hundred feet to the right and follow the same downhill course, both of us using our compasses to ensure we followed a precise direction as we moved down.

We gathered up the tools of the stand examiner - maps and compass and aerial photos for orientation. This also included the metal measuring tapes for determining the diameter of trees; D-tapes we called them. We packed up the increment borers for drilling into the center of the tree for extracting a small, pencil thin core sample for counting growth rings and determining the approximate age of the tree. There was also a visual sighting device called a Relaskope that allowed for several things. It enabled us to determine which trees we would actually measure when establishing a plot by providing a guide for trunk size and proximity. It also contained an inclinometer device so that we could measure both the slope of the ground we stood on and the height of the trees we were measuring. Additionally there were notebooks and paper and plastic flagging and of course, lunch. With all of this loaded into my vest pockets and pack, and with my cork-boots laced up tight, I stepped off the edge of the road and into the biggest collection of bear poop I had ever seen in my life.

It was everywhere – in small mounds and great piles. There were piles on top of stumps and little collections alongside the huckleberry bushes. I called to Stan who was about to step off the road just downhill from me.

"Watch out for bears", I shouted. He stopped, smiled, waved and stepped into the woods. Maybe I had cried 'bear' once or twice before jokingly.

"Stan!" He looked again.

"Bear shit," I pointed at the ground. He waved again and disappeared.

Although there have been reports in the last few years of grizzlies in the far North Cascades, actual sightings are extremely rare. There is a recently confirmed report that includes a photo. But at the time I waded through this pile of bear poop, I had not heard of such sightings and so I assumed these would be black bears. They're smaller and a bit less aggressive than a grizz', but they are still bears. Knowing this, I walked carefully. Quietly. With my eyes open.

It wasn't two minutes before I saw movement down the hill directly ahead of me. The ground was so steep it was easier sitting down than to try to stand and look. And so, seated, I began watching the movement below me. After some time I could make out that there were two bears. They were still quite distant and the wind was blowing upslope as the morning air heated in the sun so I felt as long as I remained distant and quiet they probably would not see me. At the time this happened, bears were reputed to have terrible eyesight, although I do not recall thinking of how close I should be able to get. It turns out that they can see at least as well as we can, but on this day I was still living with the old, and incorrect information.

It became obvious in a short while that these two were digging around the stump of a dead tree, probably looking for grubs and such in the rotting bark. Black bears are known to be very non-particular diners, eating pretty much anything they can shove into their mouths, be it animal, vegetable, or tree bark. Early in the year, they cause considerable damage to young replanted areas by peeling the sweet, soft bark from fir trees and eating the cambium - the moist, sweet growing part of the tree. The girdled trees often die as the routes of transportation between needles and root are severed. Today's menu, though, seemed to be bugs.

After a few minutes, the bears rooted their way behind the stump and disappeared from view. I sat still long enough to convince myself that they were not coming back and I moved on down to follow them.

Moments later, moving slowly, I spotted them again, this time, however, counting three furry beasts and realizing the two I had seen previously were not as far away as I first thought. They were cubs but I had not seen the mother with them at first. As I observed them earlier through the brush, what I had taken to be an effect of distance was just their small size.

Is there anyone who has not heard of the danger of a mother bear with cubs? Stories abound that describe the mother savagely defending her young from all sorts of perceived threats. I had immediate visions of momma bear on her back feet, snarling, forelegs slashing at me just before she fell on me and closed her jaws around my skull. I realize that the animal I saw probably weighed only a couple of hundred pounds or so, not that much more than me, but that's two hundred bear pounds. I have always viewed bear pounds as measured sort of like dog years. One bear pound counts for about seven human pounds so any hand-to-hand contest between the bear and me would be sort of like wrestling a fourteen hundred pound Hulk Hogan. With claws.

There is a difference between seeing a bear in the zoo and one in the wild. I realize that that is an obvious statement but I must make it. My former brother-in-law was a keeper at the zoo in Seattle and a number of years ago he took me to visit Ruff, the resident grizzly. We fed Ruff oranges through the window in the back of his cage and even with the one-inch thick bars between us, it was frightening to see the enormous face just a couple of feet away. He was not in a bad mood either. I shiver to imagine stumbling onto an animal his size in the mountains. In the woods, you look in all directions and realize there is nowhere to hide. Even a small bear causes my heart rate to increase considerably. I've always heard that the real difference between a black bear and a grizzly bear is that the black bear will climb the tree to get to you, while the grizzly will simply shake it until you fall out.

With these disturbing thoughts spinning around in my head, I examined my options. First, I could just leave. That would mean, though, I would miss the chance to observe these animals first hand, and wasn't my degree in wildlife biology? Wasn't this exactly what I had studied to do? With my training and experience, shouldn't I be able to follow these three bears at a distance and watch without being detected? Was I a coward? Rationalization completed, I followed.

For perhaps twenty minutes, I continued to stay about the same distance from mom and her cubs. I watched from behind tree trunks, until the three of them dropped over the edge of the ravine we were following downhill - the boundary of the stand of timber that I was supposed to be surveying. Creeping slowly, I made my way to the edge of the ravine and dropping to my stomach, I eased my head over the edge to try to locate them. I saw all three immediately, at the bottom of the ravine, about two hundred feet from me. The cubs had climbed onto a log that was lying crossways just above the stream that cascaded down. As I watched them, I felt as though I was transported back to my childhood. When I was about eight years old, I saw my first Walt Disney True Life Adventure at the movies. I don't recall the name of the film but I do remember the theater and the narrator describing the scene as two bear cubs wrestled in a tree. As I watched the real-life version of the film, one of the cubs lost his footing and tumbled into the stream. It was a delightful scene. As all of this was going on, mom continued across the stream and had climbed to the top of the other side and disappeared. The cubs had set up a near-continuous bleating sound that probably served to keep mom aware of their location. Any change in the sound would immediately alert her to a problem. It was a bit like a sheep bleat and I could just hear it over the rush of the water.

I knew this event was just too good to keep to myself, and with mom temporarily out of sight, I rose and moved as quickly as I could in the opposite direction, searching for Stan. It took only a few minutes to find him and tell him what I had discovered and shortly we were both on our bellies, crawling to the edge of the ravine. The cubs were still there, still playing in the water and on the log - still as entertaining as when I have first spotted them down the hill. As we smiled and laughed quietly, whispering to one another, I began looking carefully for some sign of the mother but saw nothing.

The slope down the ravine angled gently at first, but then dropped steeply to the bottom, thus creating an area we could not see at the very bottom of the ravine. The cubs were still making their bleating sounds as they started up the hill in our direction and disappeared into the blind spot below us. As they left our view a terrifying thought came to me that the mother could well be coming back up this side of the ravine, having re-crossed while I was finding Stan. My smile left as I looked at my partner and said, "I don't know where the mother is." As he looked at me, his face went white and his eyes grew large. I could tell that he had the same thought as me. We had just started to back slowly away from the edge of the ravine, still on our stomachs, when at that exact instant a head popped over the edge, about three feet away from me. My heart stopped, then began pounding and before I could even think, we were both on our feet running as fast as the steep terrain would allow. Ready for the sight of a ferocious mother, we instinctively fled. Seconds later, we were both howling with laughter. It was one of the cubs who had climbed the slope and poked his tiny little head into our view.

I still have the image clearly in my mind to this day. The tiny little bear face - they couldn't have been but a few weeks old - eyes flung open in terror as he saw us. I have to wonder if that bear sits around at night and laughs to himself about the two terrified humans he chased away that morning down on Bacon Creek.

The Dumb Luck Fire

Project fires - wildfires in other words - are always given names for reference and reporting and, I suppose, for management purposes. I guess it would be a lot harder to say "that fire that's up the 3032 road about twelve miles and then northeast over the ridge about..." Well, you get the idea. When we stumbled onto this particular blaze, quite by accident, it was named the "Dumb Luck" fire. Supposedly that was because it was pure dumb luck we found it, although I have always wondered if it was meant to cast aspersions on our character for being in such a place on such a day. Or perhaps this is just the cleaned up version of the fire name that so aptly described our circumstances that day.

Dan and I had been working for a few weeks on a several thousand acre timber stand exam for the Forest Service. Timber stand exams, or TSE's, as they were called, were my absolute favorite work in the woods. They almost always involved large tracts of land, unlike the smaller designated timber sale areas, and they were usually done in beautiful old-growth timber. The purpose of the TSE was to gather a general picture of the size and density and general vigor of the trees growing in the area. It was always pleasant because it involved leaving the road some distance behind and hiking through the woods, wondering if we were the first people to ever be on that particular spot.

This TSE contract on the Tieton Ranger District of the Wenatchee National Forest and was located between White Pass and Yakima. It was beautiful, high elevation east side Cascade forest. The walk in was a few miles by ridge top trail past a deep, south facing drainage called Thunder Creek. On this hot August day, the name was appropriate as late afternoon thunderstorms built up and then unleashed a furious barrage of lightning and, you guessed it, thunder. On our storm-induced retreat from the distant stand of timber on Shellrock Peak, we followed the same ridge top trail and were hopelessly exposed to the weather and wearing the safety shoes of all good timber people, steel spiked caulked boots. We called them corks. They were heavy leather boots that laced up to mid-calf and held several dozen one-quarter inch long steel spikes protruding from the soles. That's right, steel. We were walking lightning rods; steel hard-hats and steel spikes. We were the perfectly grounded conduction mechanism, although we could rest assured in our ability to grip the tops of fallen logs with these sticky shoes, secure in our position. We would be able to avoid falling off the logs we walked atop as the lightning blasted us to bits.

Walking this ridge top, we watched to the south across the Tieton River as the storm rolled east along Rimrock Lake and to the vertical faces of Kloochman Rock. There were dozens of bolts hitting the ground but all were hidden to one degree or another by clouds or rain or intervening ridge lines. There was one bolt, one particularly brilliant bolt that found a tree about a mile distant and clearly in view from where I stood. For all the years that I have spent working outdoors and through all of the storms I have weathered, this was the most remarkable event I have ever witnessed. I happened to be looking at exactly the right place, which was the very tree this bolt of lightning chose to hit.

The streak of lightning from cloud to ground, the explosion of light from red-orange to white; the pieces of tree thrown into the air, it was all over in two or three seconds. It was so dramatic that I didn't move for a bit as the sight was still visible in my retinal image. Mouth open, I turned and looked at Dan. His jaw was hanging as well. There was nothing to say but we both had enormous grins as we raced for the trail head and the relative safety of the truck.

The storms subsided later that evening and tuned into a light but steady drizzle. It rained all night.

The next morning found us a few miles to the southwest of our prior day's location. We drove to the road end and walked in on a trail that climbed a ridge that ran east to west - Russell Ridge. Using maps and aerial photos, we navigated in to a predetermined start point, hung the necessary plastic flagging to mark the entry point for the Forest Service inspectors who would follow us, and started two parallel cruise lines along the north facing slope of the ridge. Dan was about mid-slope while I was about two hundred feet from the bottom while we worked our way in a westerly direction through the wet undergrowth.

We were not working for more than fifteen minutes before I smelled smoke. There's a quality to the aroma of a fire in the forest that is at once as pleasantly appealing as a fireplace in winter and as yet as unfriendly as the reality of the wildfire. It's not like smelling wood smoke from winter warming fires in the houses of your neighborhood. It smells wild.

Garbed in metal hard hat and rubber rain gear, I continued moving west; and continued smelling smoke but could see nothing. The clouds were on the deck. We were in them. The rain continued. I thought I heard something. Dan? It sounded as though he was calling me, but he was barely audible. I took off my hard-hat to eliminate the noise of the rain hitting it, and listened. Nothing. I waited. Then, it came so faintly I wasn't sure I really heard it.

"Denny!" It was Dan.

With a rough bearing on the sound, slightly behind me and uphill, I started toward my partner. It only took about ten minutes to find him and the source of the smoke smell. It was not the bolt that we had seen yesterday but a brother to it that had struck and shattered an old ponderosa pine. The top had been blown completely out and pieces of it lay everywhere, some as much as two hundred feet away. Most of the pieces showed signs of fire, but as scattered as they were any that had been burning had been extinguished by the rain. The main trunk, though, was vigorously on fire.

We had no tools at all to work with, so we strung the blue and white plastic flagging we used to mark our survey boundaries entirely around the perimeter of the blaze. It was impossible to miss no matter the direction from which you arrived. Knowing that the trail we had entered from lay along the ridge directly above us, we flagged a route straight to the top and intersected the trail where we once again stretched flagging that would not be missed. Then out we hiked, back to the road.

Driving down the mountain, in the rain, I felt a little odd about calling in a fire. So did the proprietor of the small grocery and fishing tackle store that we reached first. This was well before the proliferation of cell phones and there were no telephone lines that far out so we made a call on his radio-telephone to the local forest service office. The store owner watched me, seeming to be amused by my conversation, while I described what Dan and I had found to the district Fire Management Officer.

"You found what?"

"Where did you say this was?"

"You marked it how?"

By this time, we were both enjoying the luxury of drying out and so rather than make the drive back up the mountain and the hike back into the timber for what would amount to less than a half days work, we opted to take the day off and spent it lounging along the river, back at camp with a fire that we built under a tree and later by driving to some nearby scenic spots we had not had time to visit before.

The following morning we went back to Russell Ridge. I could hear the music when we were still a mile away. It made sense to hike back along the trail to our flag line, follow it down to the fire, and then resume our survey from where we had stopped the day before. We knew that even though it was technically a "wildfire", this small burn would not spread very far, particularly with the crack troops of the Forest Service on the job.

We found the flag line with little trouble since the music was from a large "boom box" which sat on a stump alongside the trail. One of the crew was stationed there to direct others in the party to the scene. He had pretty nice duty that day since his job consisted of sitting in the sun on a beautiful day and waiting for anyone who wandered along and needed directions. Down the hill we went, following the flagging that we had hung the day before.

It didn't take long to reach the scene going downhill and we found four people busily digging with shovels and Pulaski's and the fire was already nearly extinguished. We paused for a few minutes to converse and discovered that it received its project name of "Dumb Luck". Laughs were had all around and something told me that the conversation back at the ranger station may have involved the changing of at least one letter as the fire crew asked themselves, "Now what kind of person would be out hiking through the woods on such a rainy day as this one?"

A6

October has always been my favorite month. I used to think it was because my birthday fell in that month and as a result it was always a bit special. Now that I'm well past half a century on the planet, I'm not so certain that the birthday thing has much to do with it. I think it's more that in the Northwest of the United States, October tends to bring a certain quality of light with it. Probably it is something to do with the angle of the sun during that period. It may also be that October tends toward periods of pleasant weather. It is a time of clear, warm days, which are always appreciated in the Northwest along with crisp, cool nights. The colors of fall begin to appear and that, taken with the softer, more golden light of autumn produce some truly spectacular vistas. Add to that the occasional light dusting of new snow on the mountains and you have a spectacular arrangement.

I remember one clear October day just east of White Pass in the Washington Cascades. I had made my way up a north bound Forest Service road to a high ridge area that served as the home for a number of towers. Radio towers and microwave towers and I don't know what all occupied a small area on the eastern end of a long rocky spine called Bethel Ridge. Running east to west at a fairly constant elevation, the ridge drops sharply off to the south and into the Tieton River drainage. The suddenness of the descent is reminiscent of the American southwest table lands. It happens dramatically from a nearly flat summit and drops over three thousand feet in about three miles. The western end of Bethel Ridge widens into an area known as Cash Prairie. This is the southern end of a mostly rolling mountainous segment that extends ten or fifteen miles to the northeast to the Naches River drainage. Much of this area, between the Tieton and Naches Rivers, is accessible only on foot. Continuing west from the Cash Prairie area, a trail follows the ridgeline until it intersects with Shellrock Peak about four miles distant. The ridge between Cash Prairie and Shellrock has a steep north face, dropping just as dramatically as the south side, into a drainage not so appealingly called Rattlesnake Creek. I have never been there so I can't testify to the appropriateness of the name, but given the implications, I do not think I'll be going.

On following the ridge to the west toward Shellrock Peak one reaches an intersection that allows the hiker to follow trails either north or south. This particular day I walked toward the south, following the trail from Shellrock for a mile or so, eventually turning to the east as the ridge bends in that direction. Upon nearing the end of all these miles of ridge walking, I was headed back in the direction from which I started and it was as though I had circled around the rim of a large bowl. Putting soup in this bowl would have produced less than spectacular results since it would have all drained away through the opening that lay in front of me. The rim was incomplete. As I stood on the edge of this great bowl, I stopped and absorbed the sight in front of me.

North and west, the declivity held the timber I was to survey, that day. East and south, the stream that drained the basin opened into a broadening valley that ultimately led to the Tieton River. West of me, I could see the looming peak of Mt. Rainier. The still early morning sky was that October, high elevation cobalt blue with not so much as a single cloud. The red and yellow maple and alder and willow were scattered in the bottom of the basin below me. The western larch, also known as tamarack, were just showing a hint of the yellow that preceded the distinctive dropping of their needles; the only conifer that is not also an evergreen. The silence was near total. I could hear no sounds. No birds. No wind. Nothing but my breathing. The air was so clear and so clean that distance became impossible to gauge. And then seemingly from nowhere - SSSHHHHGGGRRRR!

The ground shook, the air screamed, the stillness vanished in an instant when from behind the ridge to my right a Navy jet - an A6 Intruder - rocketed past, flying lower than where I stood. I looked down on it, into the bubble of the canopy seeing a glint of white helmets as the two side by side occupants shot past me traveling at high speed, entering through the opening in the bowl, heading north directly at the ridge to my left. At barely one hundred feet from the treetops, the howling aircraft seemed headed toward disaster, but at the last instant the nose lifted and the craft skimmed just above the trees, cleared the ridge trail I had just walked less than an hour before, and as it passed barely above the trail the pilot rolled the aircraft upside down, shoved the nose over and it dropped, inverted, into the Rattlesnake Creek drainage. The sound faded abruptly, ricocheting off the sides of the valleys beyond my sight. In a matter of probably five seconds, this aircraft had appeared from total silence and then departed in the echoes of its arrival. Within another fifteen seconds, it was again totally silent, the pilot having driven his vehicle into the lower reaches of the canyon beyond. I heard no more.

The sky was still an unbroken cobalt field. The air was still as clear as crystal. The echo in my mind of the thunderous roar was all that remained, making me wonder if I had actually seen that streaking jet fly past me or if I only imagined it.

Bush Vet

It was August and hot even in the mountains. The only place that any relief could be found was in the heavy shade of the timber along the river bottoms. That was where I saw him - along one of the rivers deep in the Cascade Mountains, miles from anywhere.

In truth that river is misnamed Sloan Creek, but in terms of water volume and grandeur and the feeling of power that it imparts it is a river. It was where I had gone to get away from the stifling heat that I had endured all day long while doing timber stand exams on contract for the Forest Service. It was rugged country with steep terrain and particularly unpleasant brush both by amount and composition. The wickedly thorned and aptly named Devils Club seemed always to be the only thing at hand just as my feet would skid out from under me and I would grab for something to hold onto. The trees were huge and the mosquitoes and no-see-ums were happily feeding on me as I worked in the heat.

For respite from all of this, I made my way to the river, intending to pick the devils club thorns from my hands with the safety pin I always kept pinned to my shirt pocket. I had my fly rod along in case there seemed an opportune spot for waiting trout.

It was after the thorns were mostly out of my hands that I noticed the huge fir tree fallen across the river upstream from where I sat. So, fishing paraphernalia at the ready, I made my way out onto the trunk of that tree with my destination - an open, gravely beach - in sight on the other side. At mid-trunk I stopped to admire the water upstream and downstream. It was while looking down the river that I noticed a movement along the stream bank not far from where I had started out a few moments before. It was a dog.

Sort of an indistinguishable, mixed breed mutt and I watched him for probably several minutes before it occurred to me to wonder "why is a dog out here?" such a long way from anywhere.

While trying to understand how this small dog was in such an out of the way place, I realized the dog was not alone. I could just make out the movement of what was clearly a person, although I could not tell who it might be since I looked at the image through a layer of brush and fir and cedar branches.

People weren't one of the common sights in the line of work I was involved in at the time and so I almost automatically turned on the trunk of the river-spanning tree and was making my way back to greet this stranger when he came fully into view.

At first, I was uncertain of whether he saw me although I was in plain view standing on the tree trunk. The noise of the river made conversation unlikely at the distance we were apart, so I made no attempt to hail him. Finally, he looked up and saw me. I looked at him. Neither of us raised a hand – we just stared at one another. He was dressed in green camouflage fatigues. His boots were laced together and hanging from around his neck as he prepared to cross the river. He had on a backpack, also camouflage green and obviously heavily loaded, and in his hand he held a rifle. A rifle that I recognized immediately, from another time. It was an M16. He looked at me. I looked at him.

Mere seconds passed as we realized that neither of us expected to encounter the other in this remote spot, and then he stepped into the river. Rifle over his head, he waded into the stream fully clothed except for his boots, his dog swimming behind him. As he passed me, maybe thirty yards away, downstream, I noted with curiosity a handmade wooden cross attached to the back of his backpack. Then he was climbing the opposite bank and without a glance back at me, disappeared into the brush of the other side.

That's when the thought struck me. Bush Vet. That's who this guy was that I had just seen. Across the river where he had gone, there were no roads and there were no trails. There was only wild country and steep mountains. Whatever he carried on his back seemed to be all that he had need of.

I've not been back to that particular spot since. Probably I never will see it again, but I can remember it so vividly in my mind. And strangely, I wonder with surprising regularity about that man.

The End – Final Thoughts

Everyone knows that it rains all of the time here. At least that's what we'd like you to believe in our attempt to discourage others from moving to this paradise on the coast. Like the West Texas sun or New York City cab drivers, it is a generalization that has at least most of its basis in fact. Some years, I think it is a fact. It starts raining by November and continues until sometime late in July.

For the most part, my life is minimally affected by the rains these days. I am inside most of the time now. That was not the case in the past, when I was working in the woods.

In those days, I often woke to the sound of rain. Rain on the roof of whatever shelter I happened to be occupying. Some days that would be at home. Others it would be on the roof of a tent if I were working in a remote area. And some days it was barely even a tent, just a sheet of plastic stretched over a rope tied between two trees. Those days were the worst. Even in the rain, the bugs somehow managed to fly. The rain never stopped the mosquitos. Mosquitos seem to prefer instrument flying conditions. After the first few weeks of a season, it seemed as if I mostly forgot about them unless they were particularly vicious for my attention.

In spite of the weather, the work was what I was there for. That and the incredible places I got to visit. I don't know how many times I have said,

"Step into my office," with a wave of my arm as I made toward a handy stump or boulder and sat while I conferred with someone. My office was, as they say, "as big as all outdoors". It was all outdoors.

Sound appealing? I know that at times it still does to me. Especially those days when I look up from my computer screen and out the window, and see the branches of the big, second-growth fir trees around the office complexes where most of my work seems to be found these days, and I feel more than just a twinge of yearning to slip on the cork boots and grab my diameter tape, increment borer, maps and aerial photos and head up the ridge to the next stand of timber that needs a good looking over. At those times, I don't think of the bugs.

For several years, I lived next door to a man who used to tell me stories of growing up and working on the Olympic Peninsula during and just after the Great Depression. Logging in those days was considered one of the ways out of poverty and if you were lucky enough to get the work, the last thing you were going to do was complain about having to work outside in the nonstop, driving rain of the Northwest. As Henry would tell it, before the advent of rubber rain gear, they wore these things called "tin pants". Essentially their jackets and trousers were made of heavy canvas that was smeared with as much pitch, gleaned from the trees they were cutting, as could be had. Boots were soaked overnight in pans filled with the oil drained from the crankcases of the loaders and yarders. The oil seeped so completely into the leather that it kept the water out. I have to wonder what it was like living in a bunkhouse full of men who had spent the day sweating in the rain and then standing their pants alongside the wood stoves to dry out. The "tin pants" title came from the stiffness that would set in on the pitch soaked canvas as it dried. And I complain about rain gear.

It's fun to let my mind wander and drift back to the distant past, imagining what it was like for the sailors on Vancouver's ship as he sailed into Puget Sound for his first look at the "luxuriant" forest. It's fun to imagine what it must have been like here, before freeways and cities, to see the coastline covered solid with timber that continued all the way to just below the summits of the mountains. And it's fun to imagine those early days of axes and oxen and finally the advent of saws and all of the many things that have happened between then and now. Technology changed the face of this country beginning all those years ago.

Looking at the forest today, it is difficult to imagine what it must have been like two hundred years ago. What I do know is that much has changed just in the years since I was one of those guys slogging through the brush. Just in that time we've grown more sensitive about what we do to our public lands. We have set aside more and more land and should be pleased with our ability to continue being able to visit the parks and wilderness areas and see and feel what it was like hundreds of years ago. But I still worry about it. Given the nature of the painful divisiveness we are experiencing in the country and the world today, I think it prudent to keep an eye on things and never assume that our forests and public lands will not be at risk. Ever since this country was settled all this has been under attack. And it has never been more at risk than right now. Keep your eyes open.

My opportunity to spend a decade being totally absorbed by the outdoor life is something I continue to deeply appreciate. The challenges of terrible weather, low wages, risk and of course, the bugs in no way reduce the satisfaction I feel at having had this opportunity. I suppose some would be puzzled by the idea that living in such continual discomfort provides me anything other than relief at having left it behind. The truth is, there has never been any work I have done that I enjoyed or appreciated more. Sure, I can look out the window at a rain and snow mix and say to myself, "well at least I'm in here where it's warm and dry", but if I am totally honest, even now I would far prefer to be lacing up a wet pair of corks and stepping off the edge of the road, almost giddy with the idea of what I might see before the end of the day.

-THE END -

Acknowledgements

I wish to extend my thanks to all those who endured endless discussions, or more correctly endless lectures, as I related these stories over campfires, during ski trips and whenever I was able to station myself between the listener and the door.

Special thanks for reading and commenting on the manuscript to Tom Frank, Dr. Berl Nussbaum and Steve Calish.

During my independent consulting days, I relied heavily on the patience and endurance of Dan Hanika. It was good for us both when you wised up and refused to spend another summer in the rain and brush. Thank you for all your efforts before you awakened to reality.

To Mike Collier, owner of Bear Paw Foresters, I appreciate you giving me the chance to get started on an adventurous part of my life.

To Pete Holmberg, thanks for taking a boy from the flatlands and turning him into a mountain man. And to Pete's "left hand man" Vern Hollo – you have no idea how much entertainment you provided me and the rest of the crew at Monte Cristo with your antics. And to the rest of that crew, all the permanent and the seasonal employees from those first two years, knowing you added much to my life.

To my family and my friends – thank you for being there and for putting up with so much.

About the Author

After receiving a BS in Wildlife Biology, Dennis worked for the U.S. Forest Service in Washington and Oregon before starting an independent business, providing contract and consultation support to government agencies as well as private landowners. Eventually, he moved his work indoors with a degree in computer science and has written on outdoor and aviation topics for magazines and newspapers. He splits his time between a cabin at Lake Wenatchee and his home in Everett, Washington where he lives with his wife and family and a collection of dogs and cats.